A Basic English Grammar

John Eastwood

Ronald Mackin

Oxford University Press

Oxford University Press
Walton Street, Oxford OX2 6DP

Oxford   New York   Toronto
Delhi   Bombay   Calcutta   Madras   Karachi
Petaling Jaya   Singapore   Hong Kong   Tokyo
Nairobi   Dar es Salaam   Cape Town
Melbourne   Auckland

and associated companies in
Berlin   Ibadan

Oxford, Oxford English and the *Oxford English* logo
are trade marks of Oxford University Press.

ISBN 0 19 432940 2

First published 1982
Tenth impression 1989

A Basic English Grammar is published by
arrangement with Cornelsen & Oxford University Press
GmbH. It is an adaptation of *A Grammar of Spoken
English* by Ronald Mackin and John Eastwood which
was first published in Germany by Cornelsen &
Oxford University Press GmbH, Berlin, in 1980.

Typeset in Linotron 202 Helvetica by
Promenade Graphics Limited, Cheltenham, England.

Printed in Yugoslavia.

Contents

Introduction

A Basic English Grammar is a reference book for students of English as a foreign language. It covers the grammatical structures and communicative functions that are generally taught in the first three or four years of English. It is therefore suitable for students up to an intermediate level.

The language described is contemporary standard British English. Some British-American differences are also included. The examples are mostly of everyday spoken English, although a smaller number are typical of formal or written style. Where necessary, usages are marked as informal/formal or as spoken/written.

The examples are printed in colour and the notes in black. The notes give basic information on form and use as simply as possible. The examples and notes are numbered whenever the notes refer to individual examples: note 1 refers to example 1, and so on.

Technical terms have been kept to a minimum, and there is a glossary of those used. There is also a full index.

Contextualized exercises on the main grammatical points in this book are printed in a companion volume, *A Basic English Grammar: Exercises,* by John Eastwood. This is published in two editions, one with a key and one without.

Key to phonetic symbols

iː	see	ʊ	good	aɪ	by
ɪ	big	uː	soon	aʊ	how
e	get	ʌ	bus	ɔɪ	boy
æ	man	ɜː	third	ɪə	near
ɑː	bath	ə	away	eə	fair
ɒ	top	eɪ	day	ʊə	sure
ɔː	saw	əʊ	go		

p	pen	f	fine	h	help
b	book	v	very	m	mine
t	time	θ	think	n	new
d	dog	ð	that	ŋ	long
k	can	s	say	l	last
g	game	z	zoo	r	room
tʃ	cheap	ʃ	shop	j	yes
dʒ	job	ʒ	measure	w	water

(r) The sound [r] is used before a following vowel.

' The next syllable is stressed, e.g. *away* [əˈweɪ].

↘ The next word has a falling intonation.

↗ The next word has a rising intonation.

1 Word order

1.1 Positive statements

	Subject	Verb phrase	
1	*Subject*	*Verb phrase*	
	Two girls	were talking.	
	My foot	hurts.	

	Subject	*Verb phrase*	*Object*
2	We	had	a marvellous holiday.
	I	can see	something.

	Subject	*Verb phrase*	*Complement*
3	Margaret	is	very nice.
	She	seems	a nice person.

	Subject	*Verb phrase*	*Adverb phrase*
4	Your friend	is	over there.
	The money	was	on the table.

The word order in a statement is

1 subject + verb phrase
2 subject + verb phrase + object ▷ 1.4
3 subject + verb phrase + complement ▷ 1.5
4 subject + verb phrase + adverb phrase

1.2 Adverbs and adverb phrases

Two girls were talking **loudly**.
Last year we had a marvellous holiday **in Italy**.
Margaret is **always** very nice.
The money was **certainly** on the table **this morning**.

We can add one or more adverbs or adverb phrases to the four sentence types in 1.1.
Adverbs and adverb phrases can come at the beginning, in the middle or at the end of a sentence. There are different rules for the different types of adverbs. ▷ 24.4

1.3 Other kinds of sentence

1 *Negative statements*
This apple isn't very nice.
The letter has not arrived.
I don't like that colour.
It must not happen again.

2 *Questions*
Where are my keys?
What have you got there?
Did the game start on time?
Will Helen be at the meeting?

3 *The imperative*
Wait here.
Don't touch anything.

4 *Exclamations*
What a beautiful day!
How stupid!

1 In a negative statement we put *n't/not* after *be, have, do* or a modal verb. ▷ 8.1

2 In a question we put *be, have, do* or a modal verb before the subject. ▷8.2
   Questions can be with or without a question word, e.g. *where, what.* ▷ 21.1

3 For the imperative ▷ 6.1

4 For exclamations ▷ 34.1

1.4 Direct and indirect objects

1
Subject	Verb	Indirect object	Direct object
Aunt Jane	gave	Sarah	a record.
She	sent	Peter	a book.

2
Subject	Verb	Direct object	Indirect object
Aunt Jane	gave	the record	**to** Sarah.
She	sent	the book	**to** Peter.

1 The indirect object without *to* comes before the direct object.

2 The indirect object with *to* comes after the direct object.

   The direct object is the thing or person to which something happens. The indirect object is the person who receives something. ▷ 18.3 direct and indirect objects

1.5   Types of complement

1
Subject	Verb phrase	Complement
I	was	ill.
That man	is	Mac.

2
Subject	Verb phrase	Object	Complement
The food	made	me	ill.
Everyone	calls	him	Mac.

1   The subject complement is used to describe the subject.
2   The object complement is used to describe the object.

1.6   Sub clauses with **when, if, because** etc.

	(*Sub clause*)	*Main clause*	(*Sub clause*)
1	When I've finished,	I'll make a cup of coffee.	
	If it's nice,	we can go out.	
2		We can go out	if it's nice.
		I bought the coat	because it was cheap.

A sentence can have one or more clauses. A sub clause can come either

1   before the main clause or
2   after the main clause.

A sub clause begins with a conjunction, e.g. *when, if, because, after*. The word order after the conjunction is the same as in a main clause, e.g. *I've finished, it's nice*.

For reported clauses and relative clauses ▷ 27.1
For that-clauses ▷ 27.3

2 Verbs: Talking about the present

2.1 The present tense of **be**

I'**m** tired. I'**m not** very fit.
Am I fat? ~ Yes, you **are**.

You'**re** in good time. You **aren't** late.
Are you ready? ~ No, I'**m not**.

Peter **is** at home, but Judy **isn't** here today.
Is he in bed? ~ No, he'**s** in the bath.
Is she out? ~ Yes, she **is**.

It'**s** July, but it **isn't** very hot.
When **is** the concert? ~ On Tuesday.

We'**re** on holiday. We **aren't** here for long.
Are we in this photo? ~ No, we **aren't**.

Those people **are** students. They **aren't** doctors.
Are they French? ~ Yes, I think they **are**.

Form

I **am**	we **are**
you **are**	you **are**
he **is**	they **are**
she **is**	
it **is**	

Short forms

'**m**	=	am		
'**re**	=	are	**aren't**	= are not
'**s**	=	is	**isn't**	= is not

For the use of short forms ▷ 39.6

Short answers

Yes, I **am**.	No, I'**m not**.
Yes, you **are**.	No, you **aren't**.
Yes, he/she/it **is**.	No, he/she/it **isn't**.
Yes, we/you/they **are**.	No, we/you/they **aren't**.

▷ 20.1 personal pronouns

2.2 The present tense of **have (got)**

1 **have got**

I'**ve got** an envelope, but I **haven't got** a stamp.
Have you **got** a pen? ~ Yes, I **have**.

Andrew **has got** a car, but his sister **hasn't**.
What'**s** the baby **got** in his mouth?
Has Susan **got** a ticket? ~ Yes, she **has**.
Has the car **got** a radio? ~ No, it **hasn't**.

The Joneses **have got** a television. We **haven't got** one.
Have they **got** a video recorder? ~
No, they **haven't**.

Form

1

I **have got**	we **have got**
you **have got**	you **have got**
he **has got**	they **have got**
she **has got**	
it **has got**	

2   **have**

I **have** two sisters. I **haven't** any brothers.
Have you any money? ~ No, I **haven't**.
Mr Hill **has** a beard.
Has Sarah many friends? ~ Yes, I think she **has**.
The house **has** four bedrooms.
We**'ve** a lot to do, and we **haven't** much time.
Have the others any ideas?

2 | I **have** | we **have** |
    | you **have** | you **have** |
    | he **has** | they **have** |
    | she **has** | |
    | it **has** | |

Short forms
've = have   **haven't** = have not
's = has   **hasn't** = has not

Short answers
Yes, I/you **have**.   No, I/you **haven't**.
Yes, he/she/it **has**.   No, he/she/it **hasn't**.
Yes, we/you/they **have**.   No, we/you/they **haven't**.

Use

We normally use *have got*, especially in speech.
have is sometimes more formal than *have got*.

▷   5.5 other uses of *have*; 5.6 USA

2.3   The present continuous tense

1   Jane **is talking** to a friend at the moment.
    The boys **are sitting** in the garden.
2   It **isn't raining** now, look.
3   What **are** you **doing** now? **Are** you **writing** a letter?
4   **Is** Richard **working** today? ~ No, he **isn't**.

Form

I **am** talk**ing**	we **are** talk**ing**
you **are** talk**ing**	you **are** talk**ing**
he/she/it **is** talk**ing**	they **are** talk**ing**

1   The present continuous tense is the present tense of *be* + the -ing form of a verb. ▷ 2.1 *be*; 38.3,5,6 spelling of the -ing form
2   In the negative *n't/not* comes after a form of *be*.
3   In questions a form of *be* comes before the subject. But ▷ 21.2
4   Short answers are with a form of *be*.

Use

We use the present continuous tense to talk about things that are happening now, at the moment.

▷   2.5; 4.5 with a future meaning

2.4   The simple present tense

Positive statements

1a   We **sit** here every evening. I sometimes **read** a book.

b   Emma **reads** the newspaper or **watches** television.

Form

I **sit**	we **sit**
you **sit**	you **sit**
he/she/it **sits**	they **sit**

1a   With *I, you, we* and *they*, we use the base form of the verb, e.g. *sit, read.*

b   In the third person singular (e.g. with *he, she* or *it*), the verb ends in *-s* or *-es*, e.g. *reads, watches.* ▷ 38.1–3,6 pronunciation and spelling

A very few verbs have an irregular pronunciation in the third person singular, e.g. *does* [dʌz], *says* [sez]. ▷40

Negative statements

2a   I **don't live** in England; I live in Scotland.

b   My friend **doesn't come** from France; he comes from Germany.

I **don't** live	we **don't** live
you **don't** live	you **don't** live
he/she/it **doesn't** live	they **don't** live

2a   With *I, you, we* and *they*, we form the negative with *don't/do not* and the base form of the verb.

b   In the third person singular we form the negative with *doesn't/does not* and the base form of the verb (without *-s*), e.g. *live.*

Questions

3a   **Do** you **like** this music? ~ Yes, it's nice.
Which record **do** you **want**? ~ This one here.

b   **Does** Jane **want** a drink? ~ No, she's got one.
How **does** she **feel** now? ~ Better, she says.

Do I like . . .?	**Do** we like . . .?
Do you like . . .?	**Do** you like . . .?
Does he/she/it like . . .?	**Do** they like . . .?

3a   In questions with *I, you, we* and *they*, we put *do* before the subject.

b   In questions in the third person singular we put *does* before the subject. We use the base form of the verb (without *-s*), e.g. *like.*

For questions with *who* and *what* asking about the subject (e.g. *Who likes this music?*) ▷ 21.2

Short answers

4   Do you think it's a good idea? ~ Yes, I **do**.
    Does Ann know the address? ~ No, she **doesn't**.

Yes, I/you/we/they **do**.   No, I/you/we/they **don't**.
Yes, he/she/it **does**.   No, he/she/it **doesn't**.

Uses of the simple present tense

We use the simple present to talk about

1   things that happen again and again, e.g. *We sit here every evening*
2   facts, things that stay the same for a long time, e.g. *I live in Scotland*
3   feelings, e.g. *I like, I want*
4   thoughts, e.g. *I think, I know*

▷   2.8 dramatic use; 4.6 with a future meaning; 11 if-clauses; 13.2 in a sub clause of future time

2.5   Present continuous or simple present? [A]

The present continuous and the simple present tenses do not have the same uses. Study carefully the differences between them.

Present continuous

1   Kate**'s listening** to the radio at the moment.
    Mr Brown **isn't working** today.

Simple present

2   She **listens** to the music programme every day.
    He **doesn't work** on Saturdays.

3a I **think** you're right.
b   Mike **wants** a sandwich.
c   He **says** he's hungry.
d   I **have** two children.
e   The camera **costs** £55.

Present continuous

1   things that are happening *at the moment*

Simple present

2   things that happen *again and again*. But ▷ 2.6–8
3   Verbs which describe actions can have a continuous or a simple form. But some verbs are normally only used in simple tenses. These are
a   verbs of thinking, e.g. *think* (= believe), *believe, agree, understand, know, remember, forget*
b   verbs of feeling, e.g. *want, wish, like, love, hate*
c   reporting verbs, e.g. *say, ask, tell, answer*
d   verbs of possession, e.g. *have, own, belong*
e   some other verbs, e.g. *cost, weigh, seem, appear, need*

Note We use *can* instead of a present tense with *see, hear* and other verbs of perception, e.g. *I can see a café over there*.

▷   28.6 after *here* and *there*

2.6   Present continuous or simple present? [B]

Present continuous
1   I**'m learning** English at evening classes this year.
Don't take that book, please. Judy**'s reading** it.

Simple present
2   My children **learn** English at school.
She often **reads** detective stories.

1   We can use the present continuous to talk about something that is happening for a limited period of time (e.g. *this year*) but is not happening just at the moment.

2   We use the simple present for something that happens over a longer period of time.

2.7   The present continuous tense with **always**

Jennifer**'s always losing** her key.
I**'m always paying** for your coffee. Why can't you pay for a change?

Form

▷   2.3. *always* comes between *be* and the -ing form.

Use

We use the present continuous tense with *always* to talk about something that happens too often.

▷   24.7 adverbs of frequency

2.8   The simple present tense: dramatic use

1   The car **stops** outside the National Bank. Three men **get** out and the driver **stays** in the car. The three men **walk** into the bank and **take** out their guns . . .

2   Ellis **throws** the ball in to Snow, but he **loses** it. Watson **gives** the ball to Tanner. Tanner **goes** past two men, he **shoots**, but the ball **hits** a Liverpool player . . .

Form ▷ 2.4

Use

We sometimes use the simple present tense
1   to tell a story, to describe the dramatic action of a play or film
2   to describe actions (e.g. in sport) while they are happening

3 Verbs: Talking about the past

3.1 The past tense of **be**

I **was** in London last week. I **wasn't** here.
Was I asleep? ~ Yes, you **were**.

You **were** rude to that woman just now. You **weren't** very polite.
Were you at the meeting yesterday? ~ Yes, I **was**.

Philip **was** at the club last night, but Ann **wasn't** with him.
Was he with Julia? ~ Yes, he **was**.
Was she at home? ~ No, she **was** at a party.

It **was** fine yesterday, but it **wasn't** very warm.
How **was** the meal? ~ Very good.

We **were** at the back. We **weren't** near the front.
Were we in France two years ago? ~ Yes, we **were**.

The early Britons **were** hunters. They **were** not farmers.
Were the Romans here? ~ Yes, they **were**.

Form

I **was**	we **were**
you **were**	you **were**
he/she/it **was**	they **were**

Short forms
wasn't = was not
weren't = were not

Short answers
Yes, I/he/she/it/ **was**.   No, I/he/she/it **wasn't**.
Yes, you/we/they **were**.   No, you/we/they **weren't**.

3.2 The past tense of **have (got)**

have got

I **had got**/I**'d got** a little money, but I **hadn't got** enough for a taxi.
Had you **got** an umbrella with you? ~ Yes, I **had**.

have

I **had**/I**'d** a little money, but I **didn't have**/I **hadn't** enough for a taxi.
Did you **have**/**Had** you an umbrella with you? ~ Yes, I **did**/**had**.

Form

had got or **had** in all persons

Short forms
'd = had   **hadn't** = had not

Short answers
Yes, I/you/he/we/they **had**.
No, I/you/he/we/they **hadn't**.
Yes, I **did** etc.

We can form negatives and questions with *had got*, with *had* or with *did*. ▷ 3.3
had is more usual than *had got*, and we normally use *did* in negatives and questions.

3.3   The simple past tense

Positive statements

1   We **enjoyed** the show last night.
    I once **worked** in a restaurant.
    The plane **landed** safely in a field.

2   I **went** to Finland about five years ago.
    She **sang** all her favourite songs.

Negative statements

Andrew **didn't stay** very long yesterday.
We **didn't get** home until midnight.

Questions

Did you **enjoy** the show? ~ Yes, we **did**.
Did she **sing** her new hit? ~ No, she **didn't**.
What time **did** you **arrive** home? ~
About midnight.

Form

1   We form the simple past tense of most verbs with
    -*ed* or -*d*, e.g. *enjoyed, worked, liked*.
    ▷ 38.3–6 pronunciation and spelling

2   Some verbs have an irregular past form, e.g. *went,
    sang*. ▷ 40
    Regular and irregular past forms are the same in
    all persons (but not *be* ▷ 3.1).

We form the negative with *didn't/did not* and the
base form of the verb (without -*ed*), e.g. *stay*.

We form questions with *did* and the base form of
the verb (without -*ed*), e.g. *enjoy*. For questions
with *who* and *what* asking about the subject (e.g.
Who enjoyed the show?) ▷ 21.2

Short answers
Yes, I/you/he/we/they **did**.
No, I/you/he/we/they **didn't**.

Use of the simple past

We use the simple past tense to talk about things
that happened at a time that is now finished, e.g.
last night, five years ago, yesterday.

We often use the simple past tense to tell a story.

▷   3.5 present perfect or simple past?

3.4   The present perfect tense

1   I**'ve cleaned** my shoes. (So they're clean now.)

2   Mr Green **has bought** a new car. (So it's his car now.)

3   Joanna **hasn't eaten** any toast. (The toast is still on the table.)

4a   **Have** you **finished** the housework? ~
b   No, I **haven't**. I'm still doing it.

5   I**'ve just written** that letter.

6a   You **haven't posted** the letter **yet**.
b   **Have** you **found** those stamps **yet**? ~ No, not **yet**.

7a   **Have** you **seen** Sarah **today**? ~
b   No, I **haven't**. I **haven't seen** her **this week**.

8a   **How long has** Ann **lived** here? ~
b   Oh, only **for six months**. She**'s been** here **since April**.

9a   **Have** you **ever eaten** rabbit? ~ Yes, lots of times. ~
b   Well, I**'ve never had** it.

Form

I/you **have** cleaned
he/she/it **has** cleaned
we/you/they **have** cleaned

1   The present perfect tense is the present tense of *have* + the -ed form (past participle). ▷ 2.2. *have*; 38.3–6 pronunciation and spelling of the -ed form.

2   Some verbs have an irregular past participle, e.g. *bought*. ▷40

3   In the negative, *n't/not* comes after *have* or *has*.

4a   In questions, *have* or *has* comes before the subject. But ▷ 21.2
b   We form short answers with *have/has*.

Note the irregular past participles of *be* and *have*:

8b   *be* → *have been*
9b   *have* → *have had*

Use

We use the present perfect to talk about

1–4   the present result of a past action

5   something that happened only a short time ago (. . . *just* . . .)

6   an action that we are expecting (. . . *yet*)

7   something that happened during a period of time that is not yet finished (. . . *today,* . . . *this week*)

8   something that began in the past and has stayed the same up to the present (. . . *for six months,* . . . *since April*)

9   something that happened during a period of time which began in the past and has gone on up to the present (. . . *ever* . . . , . . . *never* . . .)

Note In British English we sometimes use the present perfect tense where Americans use the simple past, e.g. *Did you find those stamps yet?*

▷   5.4 *been to* and *gone to*

3.5   Present perfect or simple past?

Present perfect

1   They**'ve opened** the new road. (So it's open now.)
2   I**'ve just got** up.
3   I **haven't seen** the exhibition **yet**.
4   It **hasn't rained today**.
5   **How long has** Mrs Peters **had** that car?
6   **Have** you **ever travelled** by plane?

Simple past

1   Yes, they **opened** it **last week**.
2   Peter **got** up **at half past six**.
3   Tom **saw** it in town **on Saturday**.
4   And it **didn't rain yesterday**.
5   Let me see. **When did** she **buy** it?
6   Yes, we **travelled** to London by plane **six months ago**.

The present perfect and simple past tenses do not have the same uses. Study carefully the differences between them:

Present perfect

1   the present result of a past action
2   a short time ago
3   something that we are expecting
4   an unfinished time
5   something that has stayed the same
6   a time up to the present

Simple past

1   a past action
2   a longer time ago
3   something that is already over
4   a finished time
5   an action that changed something
6   a time in the past

We use the simple past (not the present perfect) with a phrase of past time which says (or asks) when something happened, e.g.

1   *last week*   4   *yesterday*
2   *at half past six*   5   *When . . . ?*
3   *on Saturday*   6   *six months ago*

3.6   The past perfect tense

Compare the tenses:

Present perfect

1   Alan's got no money. He**'s spent** it all.

Past perfect

2   Alan had no money last Sunday. He**'d spent** it all.
I didn't go to see the film last night because I**'d seen** it before.
Had Mrs Williams already **arrived** when you got to the station? ~ No, she **hadn't**.
After we **had looked** round the museum, we went to a restaurant.

Simple past

3   We **looked** round the museum, and then we **went** to a restaurant.

Form

had + the **-ed** form (past participle)

Some past participles end in -*ed*, and some are irregular. ▷ 40

Short forms   **'d** = had   **hadn't** = had not
We form short answers with *had*. ▷ 3.2

Use

1   Remember that we use the present perfect tense to talk about the present result of a past action.

2   When we talk about the past, we sometimes talk about one thing that happened before another. We use the past perfect tense for the thing that happened *first* and the simple past tense for what happened *later*.

3   When one thing happened and then another, we can also use the simple past tense for both actions.

3.7   The past continuous tense

Compare the present continuous and past continuous:

1   What **are** you **doing**? ~ I'**m waiting** for a bus.

2   What **were** you **doing** at six o'clock yesterday evening? ~ I **was waiting** for a bus.

Compare the past continuous and simple past:

3   We **were watching** the news when the telephone **rang**.
The accident **happened** while they **were coming** down the mountain.
What **were** you **doing** when the policeman **came**? ~ I **was** just **making** some coffee.

4a   When the telegram arrived, I **was packing** a suitcase.

b   When the telegram arrived, I **packed** a suitcase.

5   It was a lovely morning. The sun **was shining**, and the birds **were singing** in the trees.

6   While everyone **was talking** and **laughing**, Martha **was crying** quietly in the kitchen downstairs.

7   She **wanted** to be a writer when I **knew** her.

Form

was/were (▷ 3.1) + the -ing form
We form short answers with *was/were*.

Use

1   Remember that we use the present continuous tense to talk about things happening now.

2   We use the past continuous tense to talk about things happening at a time in the past, e.g. *at six o'clock yesterday evening*.

| 5.55 | 6.00 | 6.05 |

I was waiting for a bus.

3   If an action was going on for some time (e.g. *we were watching the news*) and a new, shorter action happened (e.g. *the telephone rang*), we use the past continuous for the longer action.

7.00   7.30
I was watching the news.

The telephone rang.

4a   We use the past continuous tense for a longer action that is interrupted. (The arrival of the telegram interrupted my packing.)

b   We use a simple past tense when one action follows another. (The telegram arrived, and then I packed a suitcase.)

5   We often use a past continuous tense to describe a scene, especially when telling a story.

6   We also use the past continuous tense for two longer actions happening at the same time.

7   Some verbs (e.g. *want, know*) are not normally used in continuous tenses. ▷ 2.5

3.8   The present perfect continuous tense

1   Peter **has been working** in the garden since ten o'clock this morning, and he's still hard at work. How long **has** he **been digging**? ~ Oh, for hours.

2   Alan, you**'ve been reading** that book all day. ~ Yes, I **have**, but I haven't finished it yet.

3   What **have** you **been doing** this afternoon, Carol? ~ I**'ve been talking** to some friends at the club.

Form

have been/has been + the -ing form
We form short answers with *have/has*. ▷ 2.2

Use

1   The present perfect continuous tense shows that an action began in the past and has gone on for some time. We often use the tense in a question with *How long . . .?* or with *for* or *since*. ▷ 25.7

2   We can use the tense to talk about an action that is still happening.

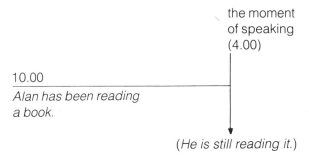

the moment of speaking (4.00)

10.00
Alan has been reading a book.

(*He is still reading it.*)

3   We can use the tense to talk about an action that finished a short time ago.

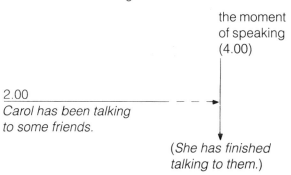

the moment of speaking (4.00)

2.00
Carol has been talking to some friends.

(*She has finished talking to them.*)

3.9   Present perfect or present perfect continuous?

1   The lawn looks nice because I**'ve cut** the grass.
(The grass is short now.)
I'm tired because I**'ve been cutting** the grass.
(The cutting went on for some time.)

2   I**'ve owned** this bicycle since I was fifteen.
(something staying the same)
I**'ve been riding** this bicycle since I was fifteen.
(something happening)

3a   Mrs Dobson **has lived** in Bristol for twenty years
and **has worked** at the bookshop for ten years.

b   Mrs Dobson **has been living** in Bristol for twenty
years and **has been working** at the bookshop for
ten years.

The present perfect and present perfect
continuous tenses do not have the same uses.
Study carefully the differences between them.

1   We use both tenses to talk about an action that
finished a short time ago. We use the present
perfect to talk about the present result of an
action, and we use the present perfect continuous
to show that an action has gone on for some time.

2   We use both tenses to talk about things that
began in the past and have gone on up to the
present. We use the present perfect to talk about
something staying the same and the present
perfect continuous to talk about something
happening.

3   We can talk about some things either as staying
the same (a) or as happening (b).

3.10   The past perfect continuous tense

Compare the two tenses:

Present perfect continuous

1   We**'ve been working** hard since seven o'clock so
we're going to have a rest now.

Past perfect continuous

2   We felt very tired yesterday afternoon because we
had been working hard since seven o'clock.
How long **had** you **been waiting** when the Browns
arrived?
Had Keith **been driving** a van before he got the
job at the factory last year? ~ Yes, he had. He**'d
been delivering** furniture for three years.

Form

had been + the -ing form
We form short answers with *had*. ▷ 3.2

Use

1   Remember that we use the present perfect
continuous tense (▷ 3.8) to talk about an action
that has gone on up to the present time.

2   We use the past perfect continuous tense to talk
about an action that went on up to a time in the
past.

3.11   **used to**

1   We **used to** live in London years ago.
2   **Did** you **use to** go cycling when you were younger? ~ Yes, I **did**.
3a   Tourists **didn't use to** come here.
b   Tourists **used not to** come here.
c   Tourists **never used to** come here.
4   Lots of tourists come here nowadays.

Form

1   *used to* + the base form of the verb in all persons.
2   We form questions and short answers with *did*.
3   The negative is
a   usually *didn't use to*
b   sometimes *used not to* or
c   *never used to* (more emphatic)

Use

used to means that something often happened in the past but does not happen now.

4   There is no present tense of *used to*. We use the simple present tense of a normal verb to talk about things that often happen these days.

Note *be used to* (+ -ing form) means to have done something so often that it no longer seems new or strange, e.g. *We're used to living in London now, but everything was new and exciting at first.*
▷ 15.5

4 Verbs: Talking about the future

4.1 will

1 Life **will** be very different in a hundred years' time. ~ Yes, it **will**, but I **won't** be here. I**'ll** be dead.
2 I think England **will** win on Saturday. ~ No, they **won't**. They **won't** beat Italy.
3 I think I**'ll** read a book this evening. Or perhaps I**'ll** watch television.

Form

will in all persons. But ▷ 4.2

Short forms
'll = will   **won't** = will not

Short answers
Yes, I/you/he/we/they **will**.
No, I/you/he/we/they **won't**.

Use

1 We use *will* to talk about something in the future (often a long way in the future). It does *not* mean that somebody has decided on an action.
2 We use *will* to talk about things which the speaker cannot control. (We use it to make predictions. ▷ 30.6)
3 If we are talking about things that we have not yet decided to do until the moment of speaking, we can use *will*. ▷ 32.1

▷ 4.4, 7, 10; 7.11; 13.2 sub clauses of future time

4.2 shall

I **shall** be ready in about half an hour.
We **shall** get wet in this rain.
I **shan't** be here next week.
We **shan't** stay long.

Instead of *will* and *won't*, we sometimes use *shall* and *shan't* (*shall not*) to talk about the future, but only in the first person.

▷ 7.11 uses of *will* and *shall*

4.3 **be going to**

1   We**'re going to** walk up the hill this afternoon.
    Are you **going to** take a picnic? ~ Yes, we **are**.
2   Look at those black clouds up there. It**'s going to** rain.
    It **isn't going to** be nice enough for a picnic.
3   We **were going to** go for a walk, but the weather made us change our minds.
    It **was** obviously **going to** rain at any moment, so they began to carry the food back into the house.

1   We use *be going to* to talk about people's intentions, things they have already decided to do in the future. ▷ 32.2 intentions
2   We also use *be going to* to make predictions when there is something in the present (e.g. *black clouds*) which tells us about the future (often the near future). ▷ 30.6 predictions
3   We use the past of *be going to* to talk about past intentions or past predictions.

4.4 **will** or **be going to**?

will

1   Trains **will** be much faster in the future.
2   Just a minute. I think I**'ll** buy a newspaper.

be going to

3   I**'m going to** read this book. I bought it last week.
4   That boat's full of water. It**'s going to** sink!

will and *be going to* do not have the same uses. Study carefully the differences between them.

We use *will*
1   to talk about things in the future which we cannot control (*not* things that we have decided to do)
2   when we are deciding to do something at the moment of speaking

We use *be going to*
3   to talk about intentions, things we have already decided to do
4   when there is something in the present which tells us about the future

4.5 The present continuous tense with a future meaning

Are you **doing** anything tonight? ~
Yes, I**'m playing** tennis. We've got a game against another club.

Are you **taking** a holiday this year? ~
Yes, we've just arranged a holiday. We**'re spending** ten days in Spain.

Form ▷ 2.3

Use

We often use the present continuous tense to talk about things that people have arranged to do in the future.

This meaning is almost the same as *be going to* used for things people have decided to do (▷ 4.3).

4.6 The simple present tense with a future meaning

What time **does** your plane go? ~
It **leaves** at half past ten on Saturday, and we **arrive** in Rome at twelve o'clock.

Form ▷ 2.4

Use

We sometimes use the simple present tense to talk about a programme or timetable in the future.

4.7 **will be** + -ing form

1 Mr Briggs is 65, so he **will be leaving** the company next month.
Will you **be staying** late at the office tomorrow? ~
Yes, I **will**. I've a lot of work to do.

2 I've got all the garden to dig—I**'ll be doing** it all day.
We're washing up now, but this time next week we **won't be washing** up—we**'ll be lying** on the beach in the sun!

1 We use *will be* + -ing form to talk about things which are fairly certain to happen in the future.
This meaning is almost the same as the present continuous tense with a future meaning. ▷ 4.5

2 We also use *will be* + -ing form to talk about actions that will be going on for some time in the future.

4.8 be to

The American President **is to** visit the Soviet Union later this year.
The two leaders **are to** meet in Moscow.
The Minister travelled to Glasgow, where he **was to** open a factory the following day.

We use *be to* for official arrangements.
We use *be to* mostly in formal written English.

▷   12.6; 31.1 *be to* used for orders

4.9 be about to

I**'m about to** leave for the station. The train leaves in twenty minutes.
I think it**'s** just **about to** start raining.
Robert **was about to** pay for the glass when he noticed a small crack in it.

We use *be about to* to talk about things which are going to happen in the very near future.

4.10 will have + -ed form

Let's go out tonight. ~ All right. I have some work to do, but I**'ll have finished** it by about eight.

Can I have the book back tomorrow, please? Will you have read it by then? ~ No, I **won't**. I **won't have read** all of it until the weekend.

We use *will have* + -ed form (past participle) to talk about something that will be completed at a time in the future.
We often use the verb *finish*.
We often use *by* and (in negative sentences), *till/until*. ▷ 25.5

5 Verbs: *be, have* and *do*

5.1 **be, have** and **do** used as auxiliary verbs

1 I'**m** writing a letter.
We'**ve** spent a lot of money.

2 I'**m not** working today.
The programme **hasn't** started yet.
You **didn't** send me a postcard.

3 **Are** you waiting for someone?
Have you filled in the form?
Does Alison take sugar?

4a Emma is coming, **isn't** she? ~ Yes, she **is**.
Peter plays golf, **doesn't** he? ~ No, he **doesn't**.

b The letter has come but the money **hasn't**.
The passengers got out and so **did** the driver.

c You *are* doing well.
I *do* like that colour.

We use *be, have* and *do* as auxiliary verbs (helping verbs). Auxiliary verbs help to form tenses.

1 In positive statements we use *be* and *have* to form tenses.

Note In two tenses only—the simple present and the simple past—we do not use an auxiliary, e.g. *I write a letter every week. We spent ten pounds.*

2 In the negative we use *be, have* or *do* (or a modal verb ▷ 7.1) + *n't/not*. ▷ 8.1

3 In questions we use *be, have* or *do* (or a modal verb) before the subject. ▷ 8.2

4 We also use an auxiliary verb (or modal verb)
a in question tags ▷ 8.5 and in short answers ▷ 8.4
b in short additions to statements ▷ 9.1
c in the emphatic form ▷ 28.2

5.2 Uses of **be**

1 Jane **is** ill. She **wasn't** at school today. She'**s been** in bed since last night.

2 She **wasn't** feeling very well yesterday, but she'**s eating** a little now.

3 This medicine **is** best **taken** after meals. It must **be taken** three times a day.

We use *be*

1 with a complement or adverb phrase ▷ 1.1; 2.1; 3.1

2 as an auxiliary verb (helping verb) in continuous tenses ▷ 2.3; 3.7, 8, 10; 7.14

3 as an auxiliary verb in the passive ▷ 10

For *be to* ▷ 4.8; 31.1

5.3   it + be and there + be

it + be

It's after one, isn't it? ~
Yes, **it is**. **It's** quarter past.
(= The time is after one o'clock.)

It wasn't expensive to go to London.
(= The fare wasn't expensive.)

Has it been very wet here?
(= Has the weather been very wet?)

It's a huge stadium, but **it'll be** full tonight.
(= The stadium will be full.)

there + be

There's no time for a meal. ~ No, **there isn't**.
(= No time exists . . . /We have no time . . .)

There weren't any trains on Sundays.
(= Trains didn't run on Sundays.)

Has there been an accident? ~ Yes, **there has**.
(= Has an accident happened?)

There'll be a big crowd here tonight.
(= A big crowd will come tonight.)

Form

After *it* the verb is always singular, e.g. *it's*.

Use

We use *it* instead of a noun phrase, e.g. *the time, the fare, the weather.*

▷   20.2 uses of *it*

Form

If the noun after *there + be* is plural, then the verb is plural too, e.g. *there weren't any trains.*

Use

We use *there + be* to say that something exists. After *there + be* we use a noun phrase, e.g. *no time, any trains, a storm,* but not usually a noun with *the.*

▷   28.6 emphatic use of *there*

5.4   **been to** and **gone to**

1   Have you ever **been to** America? ~
    Yes, I went to New York two years ago.
2   Is Judy in America? ~
    Yes, she's **gone to** Los Angeles. She'll be back next week.

We sometimes use the past participle of *be* instead of the past participle of *go.*

1   *been to* = gone somewhere and now come back
2   *gone to* = gone somewhere and still there

5.5   Uses of **have**

Auxiliary verb

1   **Have** you **sold** your car? ~
    Yes, it **had done** 100,000 miles, you know.

have (got)

2   You **had** a telephone last year. ~
    Yes, but we **haven't got** one now.

have (got) to

3   **Have** you **got to** clean the stairs? ~
    Yes, we **have to** wash the hall floor, too.

Normal verb

4   I**'m having** a sandwich.
    I think I**'ll** just **have** a cup of tea.

5   **Are** you **having** a good holiday?
    We**'ve had** some lovely weather lately, haven't
    we?

6   Did you **have a look** at the pictures?
    The children **didn't have a ride** on the donkey.

1   *have* as an auxiliary verb (helping verb) in perfect
    tenses. ▷ 3.4, 6, 8, 10; 4.10; 5.1; 7.15

2   *have* (*got*) meaning *own* or *possess*. ▷ 2.2; 3.2;
    5.6

3   *have* (*got*) *to* meaning the same as *must*. ▷ 7.4

    have as a normal verb with other meanings, e.g.

4   *eat* or *drink* ▷ 31.1 ordering food; 33.1 offering
    food

5   something happening to us, something that we
    experience

6   *have a look* = look (verb); *have a ride* = ride
    (verb) etc.

Note The normal verb *have* can have a continuous
form (*Are you having . . .?*) and we form questions
and negatives with *do* (*Did you have . . .?*)

▷   10.8 *have something done*

5.6   **have** in American English

1   GB: **Have** you **got** a ticket to London? ~
             Yes, I **have**. But my friend **hasn't got** one.

2   USA: **Do** you **have** a ticket to New York? ~
              Yes, I **do**. But my friend **doesn't have** one.

1   *have got* is more usual in British English (but we
    also use *have* especially in the past tense ▷ 3.2).

2   *have* is more usual in American English.
    Questions, negatives and short answers are with
    do.

▷   7.4 *have* (*got*) *to*

5.7   Uses of **do**

Auxiliary verb

1   What **does** this word mean? ~ I **don't** know.
    Did you learn English at school? ~ Yes, I **did**.

2   **Don't** shout. I can hear you all right.

Normal verb

3   What do you **do** in your free time?
    What are you **doing** now?
    I **did** something interesting yesterday.
    What did you **do**?

4   We're **doing** a few odd jobs.
    Mike's **done** some wallpapering.

1   As an auxiliary verb (helping verb) in the simple present and simple past tenses. ▷ 2.4; 3.3

2   As an auxiliary verb with the negative imperative. And ▷ 6.1

3   As a normal verb, to talk about an action when we do not know or do not say what the action is.

4   As a normal verb meaning e.g. *work at, finish*. ▷ 15.4

Note We use the auxiliary verb *do* with the normal verb *do* in the simple present and simple past tenses, e.g. *What do you do? What did you do?*

6 The imperative and *let's*

6.1 The imperative

1 **Come** here, please, David.
  Go and **stand** over there, Jane.
2 **Help** me with these cases, you two.
3 **Don't drop** the glass.
4 **Do** be careful.
5 **Have** a drink. ~
  Not for me, thanks. But **you have** one.
6 **Go** straight ahead here and then **turn** right at the crossroads.

Form

1 The imperative is the base form of the verb.
2 We use the same form to talk to two or more people.
3 We use *don't* in the negative.
4 We use *do* for emphasis. ▷ 28.2
5 We sometimes use *you* before the imperative.

Use

We use the imperative
1,2 to give orders ▷ 31.1
3,4 to give warnings ▷ 31.7
5 for informal offers or invitations ▷ 33.1,2
6 to tell someone how to do something ▷ 31.6

▷ 8.5 question tags; 12.6 reporting orders

6.2 let's

1 **Let's** sit down for a minute.
2 Oh, **don't let's** stop/**let's not** stop now.
3 **Do let's** finish the job first.

Form

1 After *let's* we use the base form of the verb.
2 We use *don't let's* or *let's not* in the negative.
3 We use *do* for emphasis. ▷ 28.2

Use

We use *let's* to make suggestions. ▷ 31.4

▷ 8.5 question tags; 33.1 *let me*

7 Modal verbs

7.1 Introduction to modal verbs

1a We **can** find the way all right.
b I **must** clean this floor.
c The key **may** be in the drawer.
2 **Can** you drive a car? ~
Yes, I **could** drive when I was seventeen.
3a I **can't** play the guitar. ~
But you said yesterday you **could** play.
b Alan **won't** be at the meeting tonight. ~
But he told me he **would** be there.
4a It isn't far. We **could** walk, **couldn't** we?
b A picnic **would** be nice. ~ Yes, it **would**.
c The rain **might** stop soon. On the other hand it **might not**.
d Why don't we get a taxi? ~
Yes, I think we ***should*** get one.
5a It's a holiday tomorrow. You**'ll be able to** have a rest.
b When the manager was away, Mr Fisher **was allowed to** use his office.
c I**'ll have to** take these library books back tomorrow.

Form

1 The modal verbs are *can, could, may, might, will, would, shall, should, ought to, must, need, dare.*
A modal verb always has the same form. There is no -*s* ending, no -*ing* form and no -*ed* form. But ▷ 7.13 *dare*
After a modal verb we use the infinitive without *to*, e.g. *find, clean, be.*
2 Modal verbs (and auxiliary verbs ▷ 5.1) come before the subject in questions.
3 Modal verbs (and auxiliary verbs) have *n't* or *not* after them in the negative.
4 We also use a modal verb (or auxiliary verb)
a in question tags ▷ 8.5
b in short answers ▷ 8.4
c in short additions to statements ▷ 9.1
d in the emphatic form ▷ 28.2

Present, past and future

2 The past form of *can* is *could.*
3 In reported speech *can, will, may* and *shall* change to *could, would, might* and *should.* ▷ 12.3
4 But *could, would, might* and *should* also have their own meanings. We use them to talk about the present and the future too.
5 To talk about ability, permission and necessity in the past or the future, we can use *be able to, be allowed to* and *have (got) to.* ▷ 7.16

Use

1 We use modal verbs to talk about, for example,
a someone's ability to do an action ▷ 7.2
b an action that is necessary ▷ 7.4
c a situation that is possible ▷ 7.7

7.2 Ability: **can, could, be able to**

1   I **can** swim.
Sarah **could** play the piano when she was very young.
If we go to town, I**'ll be able to** do some shopping.
Jim **can't** drive.
Can your sister dance? ~ Yes, she **can**.

2   The children fell into the water, but luckily they **were able to** hold on to the boat.
I **was able to** swim back and get help.

3   **Could** you lift the cupboard? ~
No, I **couldn't**. It was too heavy.
Were you able to paint the windows? ~
No, I **wasn't**. It rained all day.

4   We **could see** a man on the roof.
I **could hear** the traffic on the main road.

5   I **couldn't** do your job. I'm not clever enough.

Use

1   We use *can* and *could* to talk about ability or opportunity.

2   We use *was/were able to* to talk about ability or opportunity + action in the past. *I was able to swim back* means that I really did swim back.
We do not use *could* to talk about a past action which really happened.

3   We can use both *could* and *was/were able to* in questions and negative sentences. (But *Could you . . . ?* is often a request. ▷ 31.2)

4   We can use *can* and *could* with verbs of perception, e.g. *see, hear. could see* = saw.

5   We can use *could* to talk about ability in a situation which we are imagining. Here *could* = would be able to. For *would* ▷ 7.9.

▷   7.8 possibility: *could*; 7.16 *be able to*

Form

	Positive	Negative
Present	**can**	**can't/cannot**
	am/are/is able to	**am not/aren't/isn't able to**
Past	**could**	**couldn't/could not**
	was/were able to	**wasn't/weren't able to**
Future	**will be able to**	**won't be able to**

Short answers with **can** *and* **could**

Yes, I/you/he/we/they **can**.   Yes, I/you/he/we/they **could**.
No, I/you/he/we/they **can't**.   No, I/you/he/we/they **couldn't**.

7.3   Permission: **can, may, be allowed to**

1   People **can** drive/**may drive**/**are allowed to** drive
a car in Britain when they're seventeen.
People **can't** drive/**may not** drive/**are not allowed
to** drive a car before they're seventeen.
My brother is sixteen. He**'ll be allowed to** drive a
car soon.
Were you **allowed to** look round the church
yesterday? ~ Yes, we **were**, but we **weren't
allowed to** take any photos.

2   **Can** I ride your bicycle, please, Jane? ~
Of course you **can**.
May I use your telephone, please, Mr Taylor? ~
Certainly you **may**.

Use

1   We use *can, may* and *be allowed to* (▷ 7.16) to
talk about permission. *may* is rather formal.

2   We use *can* or *may* to ask permission. ▷ 31.3

Form

	Positive	*Negative*
Present	**can**	**can't/cannot**
	may	**may not**
	am/are/is allowed to	**am not/aren't/isn't allowed to**
Past	**was/were allowed to**	**wasn't/weren't allowed to**
Future	**will be allowed to**	**won't be allowed to**

We use short answers with *can/can't* (▷ 7.2) and
with *may* (▷ 7.7).

7.4   Necessity: **must, have (got) to, needn't, mustn't**

Necessity

1   I'm late. I **must** hurry.
You **must** tell me the truth.
I'**ve got to**/I **have to** go to work today.
Martin **has got to** see/**has to** see the doctor.
We **had to** wait half an hour for the bus.
I'**ll have to** go and get some eggs.

No necessity

2   **Have** we **got to** pay/**Do** we **have to** pay now? ~
No, we **haven't**/**don't**.
You **haven't got to** answer/You **don't have to**
answer the letter.
We **didn't have to** book a table.

3   I **needn't** wash this shirt. It's clean.
You **needn't** come if you don't want to.

Not allowed

4   You **mustn't** open other people's letters.
I **mustn't** forget my key.

Form

	Positive	*Negative*
Present		**needn't/need not**
	must	**mustn't/must not** ▷ 7.5
	have/has to	**don't/doesn't have to**
	have/has got to	**haven't/hasn't got to**
Past	**had to**	**didn't have to**
Future	**will have to**	**won't have to**

Short answers with **must, needn't** *and* **mustn't**
Yes, I/you/he/we/they **must**.
No, I/you/he/we/they **needn't**.
No, I/you/he/we/they **mustn't**. ▷ 7.5

Use

1   Necessity means that you cannot avoid doing
something. *You must buy a ticket* = You cannot
go without a ticket.
We use *must* and *have (got) to* to talk about
necessity.
must expresses the authority or feelings of the
speaker, and *have (got) to* (▷ 7.16) refers to the
authority of another person or to something the
speaker cannot control. ▷ 31.1 orders

2   We use the negative forms of *have (got) to* when
there is no necessity.

3   We can also use *needn't* when there is no
necessity.
Note We also use the normal verb *need* with *to*,
e.g. *Do we need to pay now? We didn't need to
book a table.* The modal verb and the full verb
have the same meaning.

4   We use *mustn't* when we are not allowed to do
something. *You mustn't forget* = Don't forget.

7.5   **needn't** or **mustn't**?

1a   The car's clean. I **needn't** wash it this week.
 b   It isn't raining. You **needn't** take a coat.
2a   The baby's asleep. We **mustn't** make a noise.
 b   Your father's very ill. He **mustn't** get up.

needn't and *mustn't* have different meanings. It is important to know the difference between them, or there can be misunderstandings.

1   We use *needn't* when there is no necessity to do something, but we can do it if we want to.
2   We use *mustn't* when we are not allowed to do something, or when there is a necessity not to do it.

7.6   Obligation: **ought to, should**

You're not fit. You **ought to** walk more.
You **should** walk more.
I **oughtn't to** eat cakes.
I **shouldn't** eat cakes.
Ought Paul **to** see a doctor? ~
Yes, I think he **ought (to)**.
Should he see a doctor? ~ Yes, I think he **should**.

Form

Positive   *Negative*
ought to   **oughtn't to/ought not to**
should   **shouldn't/should not**

Short answers
Yes, I/you/he/we/they **ought (to)**.
No, I/you/he/we/they **oughtn't (to)**.
Yes, I/you/he/we/they **should**.
No, I/you/he/we/they **shouldn't**.

Use

Obligation means that something is the right thing to do. *You ought to walk* = Walking is the right thing for you to do.
We use *ought to* and *should* to express obligation or to give advice. ▷ 31.5
There is little difference between *ought to* and *should*, but *ought to* is sometimes a little stronger than *should*.

▷   7.12 other uses of *should*; 35.1, 2 approving and blaming

7.7   Possibility: **may, might**

1   The keys **may** be/**might** be in one of those drawers.
2   Amanda **may not/might not** come tomorrow.
3   Do you think it'll snow? ~ Yes, it **may/might**.

Form

Positive   *Negative*
may   **may not**
might   **might not/mightn't**

Short answers
Yes, I/you/he/we/they **may**.
No, I/you/he/we/they **may not**.
Yes, I/you/he/we/they **might**.
No, I/you/he/we/they **might not/mightn't**.

Use

We use *may* and *might* to talk about

1   possibility in the present
2   possibility in the future
    There is little difference between *may* and *might*, but a speaker who uses *might* is a little less sure.
3   To ask questions, we use *Do you think . . . ?* and *will*.

▷   7.15 possibility in the past; 30.5 being sure and unsure; 32.2 intentions

7.8   Possibility: **could**

1   The keys **could** be in one of those drawers.
2   We **could** go out later, **couldn't** we? ~ Yes, why not?

Form

Positive   **could**
Negative   **couldn't/could not**

For short answers ▷ 7.2

Use

We use *could* to talk about

1   possibility in the present (*could* is rather less sure than *may* or *might* ▷ 7.7)
2   possibility in the future, especially in suggestions ▷ 31.4
    For the use of *could* to talk about past ability or about a situation which we are imagining ▷ 7.2

▷   7.15 possibility in the past; 31.2 requests

7.9   Imagining situations: **would**

A holiday in the Bahamas **would** be nice. ~
Yes it **would**. I**'d** certainly enjoy a holiday right
now.
How much **would** it cost? ~
I don't know, but it **wouldn't** be cheap.

Form

would in all persons.

Short forms
'd = would   **wouldn't** = would not

Short answers
Yes, I/you/he/we/they **would**.
No, I/you/he/we/they **wouldn't**.

Use

We use *would* to talk about a situation which we
are imagining (= thinking about) but which is not
really happening.

▷   7.12 other uses; 16.2 *would like*; 30.8 having
ideas

7.10   Certainty: **will, must, can't**

He left half an hour ago, so he**'ll** be home by now.
(= he is certainly home by now)
No one's answering the phone. They **must** be out.
(= They are certainly out.)
This story **can't** be true.
(= It is certainly untrue.)

We use *will, must* and *can't* to say that something
is logically certain.

▷   30.5 being sure and unsure

7.11 Uses of **will** and **shall**

will

Future	Juliet **will** be 20 next month.	▷ 4.1
Deciding	I think I**'ll** buy it.	▷ 4.1
Requests	**Will** you shut the window, please?	▷ 31.2
Invitations	**Will** you/**Won't** you sit down?	▷ 33.2
Promises	I **will** write, I promise.	▷ 32.5
Refusing	The car **won't** start. What's wrong with it?	▷ 32.4
Certainty	I sent the parcel last week, so they**'ll** have it by now.	▷ 7.10
Strict orders	You**'ll** do as I tell you.	▷ 31.1

shall

Suggestions	**Shall** we go out this evening?	▷ 31.4
Offering	**Shall** I carry your bags for you?	▷ 33.1
Promises	You **shall** have the goods by next week.	▷ 32.5
Future with **I/we**	I **shall** be on holiday in July.	▷ 4.2

7.12 Uses of **would** and **should**

would

Imagining situations	It **would** be nice to have a party here one weekend.	▷ 7.9
	If I had a lot of money, I**'d** travel round the world.	▷ 11.1
Wishing	I**'d** like to meet your brother.	
	I wish this rain **would** stop.	▷ 34.5
Requests	**Would** you write your address here, please?	▷ 31.2
Invitations	**Would** you like to come to dinner?	▷ 33.2
Preferences	I**'d** rather have tea than coffee.	▷ 34.6
Reporting **will**	She said she **would** come tomorrow.	▷ 12.3

should

Obligation	We **should** help other people.	▷ 7.6
Advice	I think you **should** go by air. It's much quicker.	▷ 31.5
In if-clauses	If you **should** be late, I'll wait for you.	▷ 11.2

7.13 dare

1   **Dare** you climb the ladder? ~ No, I **daren't**.
    I **daren't** go near the dog.
    The guests **dared not** complain.

2   **Do** you **dare (to)** climb the ladder? ~ No, I **don't**.
    I **don't dare (to)** go near the dog.
    The guests **didn't dare (to)** complain.

Form

1   We can use *dare/dared* as a modal verb.
    We use the infinitive without *to* after the modal verb.

2   We can use *dare* as a normal verb with *do/did*.
    We use the infinitive with or without *to* after the normal verb.

Use

dare means not to be afraid to do something.
We use *dare* mostly in questions and negative sentences.

7.14 Modal verbs + **be** + -ing form

Obligation
Why are you sitting here watching television?
You **ought to be doing/should be doing** some work.

Possibility
Elaine **may be coming/might be coming** to tea tomorrow.

Certainty
What's that noise? ~ It's Mr Greaves. He **must be repairing** his motorbike.

Imagining
I'm glad it's a holiday. I**'d be working** if it wasn't.

We can use a modal verb + *be* + -ing form to talk about obligation, possibility, etc.

▷   4.7 *will be* + -ing form

7.15 Modal verbs + **have** + -ed form

Necessity
Not many people came to the party—we **needn't have bought** so much food. (= It was not necessary to buy so much food, but we had bought it.)

Obligation
Peter and Susan didn't come. They **ought to have told/should have told** us. (= They had an obligation to tell us, but they didn't tell us.)

Possibility
They **may have forgotten/might have forgotten** about it. (= It is possible that they forgot about it.)

But Susan mentioned the party yesterday. She **couldn't have forgotten** about it. (= It isn't possible that she forgot about it.)

Imagining
It **would have been** nice to see them here. (= . . . if we had seen them here.)

We use a modal verb + *have* + -ed form (past participle) to talk about necessity, obligation etc. in the past.

Note We *needn't have bought* so much food. (= We bought too much.)
We *didn't need to buy* much food. (= We didn't buy much because there was no need.) ▷ 7.4

▷   4.10 *will have* + -ed form; 11.1 if-clauses

7.16 **be able to, be allowed to** and **have (got) to**

1 *Simple tenses*
I**'m able to** visit my father quite often.
The visitors **were allowed to** go inside.
You **don't have to** wait.

2 *Perfect tenses*
I **haven't been able to** find their address.
We**'ve had to** sit here in the dark all evening.
Children **had** always **been allowed to** play on the grass before.

3 *After* **will, may** *etc.*
We**'ll be able to** have a rest soon.
I **may have to** go to the bank.
They **might not be allowed to** leave early.
You **ought to be able to** find the answer.

1 We can use *be able to* (▷ 7.2), *be allowed to* (▷ 7.3) and *have (got) to* (▷ 7.4) in the simple present and simple past tenses.

2 We can also use them in the present perfect and past perfect tenses.

3 We can also use them after *will* and other modal verbs.

8 Negatives, questions and tags

8.1 Negative statements

1a I'm **not** leaving yet. I **haven't** packed my bag.
 b We **can't** stop now or we **won't** get there in time.
 c I **don't** remember that party. I **didn't** go to it.
2a There are **no** lights on.
  (= There aren't any lights on.)
 b Peter isn't here, and **neither** is Jane.
  (= Peter isn't here, and Jane isn't either.)
 c There was **nobody** in the house.
  (= There wasn't anybody in the house.)
 d I've **never** been here before.
  (= I haven't ever been here before.)

1 In a negative statement we use *n't/not* after
a the auxiliary verbs *be* or *have* ▷ 5.1
b a modal verb ▷ 7.1
c the auxiliary verb *do* in the simple present and
  simple past ▷ 2.4; 3.3
2 We can also make a negative statement with
a *no* and *none* ▷ 20.23
b *neither* and *nor* ▷ 9.1; 20.23; 27.5
c *no one, nobody, nothing* and *nowhere* ▷ 20.16
d *never* ▷ 24.7

8.2 Questions

Yes/no questions

1 **Are** you looking for someone?
 Has the new supermarket opened yet?
2 **Shall** we have lunch now?
 Will John have time?
3 **Do** you normally come here?
 Did you see Jennifer yesterday?
4 You saw Jennifer yesterday?

Wh-questions

1 Where **are** you going?
 Which book **have** you read before?
2 How **can** we get there?
 When **must** you be back?
3 Why **does** Mr Gray leave so early?
 Who **did** you see in George Street?
 (You saw somebody.)
5 Who **saw** you in George Street?
 (Somebody saw you.)

In questions we put one of these verbs before the
subject:
1 the auxiliary verbs *be* or *have* ▷ 5.1
2 a modal verb ▷ 7.1
3 the auxiliary verb *do* in the simple present and
  simple past ▷ 2.4; 3.3 (but see note 5)
1–3 Yes/no questions begin with an auxiliary or modal
  verb, and we can answer them with *yes* or *no.* ▷ 8.4
  Wh-questions begin with a question word (▷ 21)
  and an auxiliary or modal verb.
4 In informal spoken English we sometimes ask a
  yes/no question by using the same word order as
  in a statement but with a rising intonation. We do
  this to check that our information is correct. ▷ 8.5
5 When *who* or *what* asks about the subject, the
  verb is the same as in a statement, e.g. *Who saw
  you . . .?* ▷ 21.2

Alternative questions

6   **Are** you going on Monday **or** Tuesday?
     Shall we have lunch now **or** later?
     Did you take a bus **or** did you walk?

6   Alternative questions begin with an auxiliary or modal verb and have *or* (▷ 27.5) before the last alternative.

8.3 Negative questions

1   Who **hasn't** arrived yet?
     Why **aren't** I on the list?

2   Why **don't** we ask Sarah to the party?
     Why **doesn't** she come on the bus?

3   You were reading that book last month. **Haven't** you finished it yet? ~ No, it's taking me a long time.
     Don't you like it? ~ Oh, yes, I like it very much.

4   **Didn't** the Romans build this road?
     (= The Romans built this road, didn't they?)

5   **Haven't** you done well!

1   We can use a question word in a negative question to ask for information.

2   We can use *Why don't/doesn't . . .?* to make a suggestion. ▷ 31.4, 11

3   A negative question can express surprise. *Haven't you finished it?* = I am surprised that you haven't finished it. ▷ 34.7

     We use *no* to agree with a negative question, e.g. *Haven't you finished it? ~ No, I haven't finished it.*

     We use *yes* to disagree with a negative question, e.g. *Don't you like it? ~ Yes, I like it very much.*

4   We can use a negative question to ask if a person agrees with a statement. ▷ 8.5

5   We can use a negative question form with a falling intonation in exclamations. ▷ 34.1

Form

In negative questions we use an auxiliary or modal verb + *n't*.

1   In the first person singular we use *aren't I?*

8.4 Answering questions

Yes/no questions

Have you seen the photos?
1 Yes.   2 Yes, I have.   3 Yes, I have seen them.
Will you be here tomorrow?
1 No.   2 No, I won't.   3 No, I won't be here.

Wh-questions

Who wants a drink?
1 Me.   2 I do.   3 I want a drink.
Where did you buy those jeans?
1 In the market.   3 I bought them in the market.

We can answer questions
1   in one word or phrase
2   often with a short answer using an auxiliary or modal verb
3   with a full sentence

     Short answers are much more usual than full sentences.

▷   31.2, 4 answering requests and suggestions; 33.1, 2 answering offers and invitations

8.5   Question tags

1a   It's lovely today, **isn't it**? ~ It certainly is.
 b   You'll be on holiday next week, **won't you**? ~
      No, we've had our holiday.
 c   Bob likes this weather, **doesn't he**? ~
      Yes, he does.
2a   We haven't had a nice summer for ages, **have
      we**? ~ No, we haven't.
 b   The dog can't get out, **can it**? ~ I don't think so.
 c   You didn't buy these drinks, **did you**? ~
      No, David did.
3   Ann isn't here. ~ Oh, she's working, **is she**?
      I won't be long. ~ You'll be back soon, **will you**?
      Jennifer was there. ~
      You saw Jennifer yesterday, **did you**?
4a   I'd better answer these letters, **hadn't I**?
 b   You'd rather sit in the garden, **wouldn't you**?
5a   Let's have some fresh air, **shall we**? I'll open the
      window, **shall I**?
 b   Open the door, **will you**?/**would you**?/**can
      you**?/**could you**?
6a   It's lovely today, ⬊ **isn't it**?
      We haven't had a nice summer for ages, ⬊ **have
      we**?
      I'd better answer these letters, ⬊ **hadn't I**?
 b   You'll be on holiday next week, ⬈ **won't you**?
      The dog can't get out, ⬈ **can it**?
      Let's have some fresh air, ⬈ **shall we**?
      Open the door, ⬈ **will you**?

Form

1, 2   We form question tags with
 a   the auxiliary verbs *be* or *have*
 b   a modal verb, or
 c   the auxiliary verb *do* in the simple present or
        simple past
        In a negative tag we put *n't* after the auxiliary or
        modal verb.
        After the verb (+ *n't*) there is a pronoun. The
        pronoun refers to the subject of the sentence.

Use

1   After a positive statement we use a negative tag to
      ask if a person agrees with the statement. ▷ 30.2
2   After a negative statement we use a positive tag to
      ask if a person agrees with the statement.
      ▷ 34.7 showing surprise
3   After a positive statement we can use a positive
      tag when we have just found out or just
      remembered some information and we want to
      ask or check if it is correct. ▷ 34.7 showing
      interest
4a   After *had better* we use a tag with *had*.
 b   After *would rather* we use a tag with *would*.
5a   After suggestions with *let's* and after offers, we
      use a tag with *shall*.
 b   After an imperative we use a tag with *will, would,
      can* or *could*.
6a   We use a falling intonation when we think the
      statement is true and we are asking someone to
      agree with it. (But he/she may disagree.)
 b   We use a rising intonation when we are not so sure
      that the statement is true. A tag with a rising
      intonation is almost the same as a real yes/no
      question. ▷ 8.2
      We often use a rising intonation in suggestions,
      offers and requests.

9 Replacing words and leaving out words

9.1 Short additions to statements

1 I like cats. ~ **So do** I./I **do, too**.
The old man is very ill, and **so is** his wife./ and his wife **is, too**.

2 We've never been here before. ~
Neither have we./**Nor have** we./We **haven't either**.
The shops won't be open, and **neither will** the banks./and **nor** will the banks./and the banks **won't either**.

3 The girls helped with the washing-up. The boys **didn't**, though.

4 My brother can't swim, but I **can**.

5 My sister's going to Japan. ~ Oh, **is** she?

1 We make positive additions to positive sentences with *so* or *too* and an auxiliary or modal verb.

2 We make negative additions to negative sentences with *neither/nor* or *either* and an auxiliary or modal verb.

We also use an auxiliary or modal verb for

3 negative additions to positive sentences

4 positive additions to negative sentences

5 short questions after statements. ▷ 34.7 showing interest

9.2 **so** and **not** after a verb

1 Someone must have stolen your bicycle. ~
Yes, I suppose **so**.

2 Will the police get it back for you? ~
I don't think **so**.

3 Will you be able to buy a new one? ~
No, I'm afraid **not**.

1 We can use *so* after some verbs instead of a whole clause. *I suppose so* = I suppose someone must have stolen my bicycle.

2 We can use *so* after the negative form of some verbs, e.g. *think, suppose, expect, imagine*.

3 We can use *not* to give a negative answer after some verbs, e.g. *be afraid, suppose, hope, believe, guess* (USA).

Note We do not use *so* or *not* after *know* or *be sure*, e.g. *Yes, I know. Yes, I'm sure*.

9.3 Leaving out words [A]

My sister plays the piano and my brother the guitar.
(= . . . and my brother **plays** the guitar.)
I like the music but not the words.
(= . . . but **I do**n't **like** the words.)
Someone's borrowed that record and I don't know who.
(= . . . and I don't know who**'s borrowed it**.)

We can leave out words instead of saying them again if the meaning is clear without them.

▷   8.4 answering questions; 14.12 the verb after *to*; 18.4 the possessive form; 20.21 quantifiers without a noun

9.4 Leaving out words [B]

Enjoying the music? ~ Sounds great.
(= **Are you** enjoying the music? ~ **It** sounds great.)

In informal speech we can leave out words from the beginning of a sentence if the meaning is clear without them.
The words which we leave out are usually a pronoun and/or an auxiliary verb.

10 The passive

10.1 The passive: simple tenses

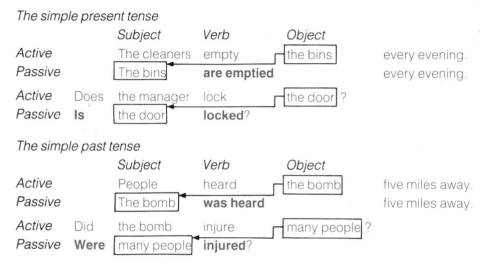

The simple present tense

		Subject	Verb	Object	
Active		The cleaners	empty	the bins	every evening.
Passive		The bins	**are emptied**		every evening.
Active	Does	the manager	lock	the door ?	
Passive	**Is**	the door	**locked**?		

The simple past tense

		Subject	Verb	Object	
Active		People	heard	the bomb	five miles away.
Passive		The bomb	**was heard**		five miles away.
Active	Did	the bomb	injure	many people ?	
Passive	**Were**	many people	**injured**?		

Form

We form the passive with *be* and the -ed form (past participle), e.g. *are emptied, is locked, was heard, were injured.*

The object of an active verb becomes the subject of a passive verb, e.g. *the bins, the door.*

If the subject of a passive verb is plural, then the verb is also plural, e.g. *the bins are emptied.*

The subject of the active verb (the agent) is left out of these passive sentences. ▷ 10.2

Use

We use the passive to make the object of the active verb more important. We put the object of the active verb at the beginning of the passive sentence because we want to talk about e.g. *the bins* not about *the cleaners*, or about *the bomb* not about *people*.

Note We can also use the past participle as an adjective to describe the result of an action, e.g. *The door is locked at the moment.* ▷ 17.1

10.2   **by** + agent

		Subject	Verb	Object	(agent)	
1	Active	The birds	eat	the food.		
	Passive	The food	**is eaten**		by	the birds
	Active	Picasso	painted	the picture.		
	Passive	The picture	**was painted**		by	Picasso
2	Active	Someone	stole	the car.		
	Passive	The car	**was stolen**.			
3	Active	The police	arrested	the driver.		
	Passive	The driver	**was arrested**.			

1   The subject of the active verb is the *agent*, the person or thing that does the action.

The agent can come after a passive verb in a phrase with *by*, e.g. *by the birds, by Picasso*.

We put in the agent if it is important to mention it.

2   We can leave out the agent if we do not know it, e.g. *The car was stolen*. (We do not know who stole it.)

3   We can leave out the agent if we do not need to mention it, e.g. *The driver was arrested*. (We know that the police arrested him or her.)

10.3   The passive: perfect tenses

The present perfect tense

Active   They have opened two new motorways.

Passive   Two new motorways **have been opened**.

Active   How much has the government spent on them?

Passive   How much **has been spent** on them?

The past perfect tense

Active   They had delivered the furniture while I was out.

Passive   The furniture **had been delivered** while I was out.

Form

We form the passive of perfect tenses with *have/has been* + past participle and *had been* + past participle.

Use ▷ 10.1

10.4　The passive: continuous tenses

The present continuous tense

Active　They're painting the bridge today.
Passive　The bridge **is being painted** today.

The past continuous tense

Active　The farmer was milking the cows when we arrived.
Passive　The cows **were being milked** when we arrived.

Form

We form the passive voice of continuous tenses with *am/are/is being* + past participle and *was/were being* + past participle.

Use ▷ 10.1

10.5　The passive: **will** and other modal verbs

Breakfast **will be brought** to your room.
Meals **cannot be served** after 11.00 p.m.
Your key **should be given** in before 11.30 a.m.
Must the bill **be paid** in cash?
The room **has (got) to be cleaned**.

Form

After modal verbs we use *be* + past participle to form the passive.

Use ▷ 10.1

10.6　The passive: direct and indirect objects

Direct object

1　They sent a telegram to the winner.
　A telegram was sent to the winner.

Indirect object

2　They sent a telegram to the winner .
　The winner was sent a telegram.

Direct object

3　They promised the workers better conditions .
　Better conditions were promised to the workers.

Indirect object

4　They promised the workers better conditions.
　The workers were promised better conditions.

The subject of a passive sentence can be either

1,3　the *direct object* of an active sentence or

2,4　the *indirect object* of an active sentence.

10.7   The passive with **get**

1   Lots of people **get injured** in the home.
    The cake **got burnt** in the oven.
    How did this clock **get broken**?

2   I had to **get dressed** in the dark.
    Without a map we soon **got lost**.
    When did they **get married**?

We use *get* in the passive instead of *be*

1   sometimes in informal English, especially to talk about something happening by accident

2   in certain expressions, e.g. *get dressed, get washed, get lost, get married*

10.8   **have/get something done**

1   **have something done**
    We **had** this room **decorated** last year.
    I**'m having** my hair **cut** tomorrow.
    Did you **have** your suit **cleaned**?

2   **get something done**
    We **got** this room **decorated** last year.
    I**'m getting** my hair **cut** tomorrow.
    Did you **get** your suit **cleaned**?

Form

1   *have* + object + past participle

2   *get* + object + past participle

    have and *get* can have a continuous form (*I'm having/getting it cut*), and questions and negatives are with *do* (*Did you have/get it cleaned?*).
    For e.g. *I had decorated this room* ▷ 3.6 the past perfect tense
    For e.g. *We decorated this room ourselves* ▷ 20.9

Use

I had/I got the car repaired = I asked someone to repair the car (and they repaired it).
get is a little more informal than *have*.

10.9   **it** + passive verb + clause

1   *Active*   People say that the company is in difficulties.
    Passive **It is said** that the company is in difficulties.

2   *Active*   They decided to appoint a new manager.
    Passive **It was decided** to appoint a new manager.

We can use *it* and the passive voice

1   before a clause with *that*. We can use these verbs: *say, think, feel, believe, know, expect, suppose, report, consider, agree, decide, arrange*

2   before an infinitive. We can use these verbs: *agree, decide, arrange*.

▷   20.2 uses of *it*

11 if-clauses

11.1 The main types of if-clause

1 Type 1: **if** + the simple present tense,
+ **will, can** or **may/might**

Probable actions in the future
If you **leave** before ten, you**'ll catch** the train.
If you **don't hurry**, you **might miss** it.
That bowl **will break if** you **drop** it.
I **can get** some more milk **if** there **isn't** enough.

2 Type 2: **if** + the simple past tense,
+ **would, could** or **might**

a *Less probable actions in the future*
If we **saved** £500, we**'d have** enough for a holiday
next year.
We **might save** enough **if** you **worked** overtime.

b *Unreal actions in the present*
If we **were** rich, I**'d travel** round the world.
We **could buy** a new car **if** you **didn't spend** so
much on clothes.

3 Type 3: **if** + the past perfect tense,
+ **would have, could have** or **might have**

Impossible actions in the past
If it **had rained** yesterday, there **wouldn't have
been** many people here.
If I **hadn't been** ill, I **could have gone** yesterday.
I **might have bought** some trousers **if** I**'d seen**
some.
Peter **would have rung** if there**'d been** anything
wrong.

1 We use Type 1 to talk about future situations that the speaker thinks are probable. *If you leave before ten* means that it is quite probable that you will leave before ten.

2a We use Type 2 to talk about future situations that the speaker thinks are possible but not very probable. *If we saved £500* means that it is possible that we will save £500 but not very probable.

b We also use Type 2 to talk about unreal situations in the present. *If we were rich* means that we are not rich.

3 We use Type 3 to talk about past situations that did not happen. *If it had rained* means that it did not rain.

Types 1–3

The if-clause can come before or after the main clause. We often put a comma when the if-clause comes first.

Note *'d* is the short form of *had* and of *would*. *If you'd asked me, I'd have told you* = If you had asked me, I would have told you.

▷ 31.7, 9 warnings and threats

11.2 Other types of if-clause

1   **if** + *a present tense,* + *the imperative*
    If it**'s raining**, take a coat.
    Don't wear those shoes **if** you **want** to go walking.

2   **if** + *the simple present tense,*
    + *the simple present tense*
    If you **mix** blue and yellow, you **get** green.
    If the temperature **falls** below zero, water **freezes**.

3   **if** + *the present continuous/present perfect tense,*
    + *a modal verb*
    If you**'re planning** a holiday, I**'ll tell** you about
    ours.
    If you **haven't been** to Wales, you **ought to go**
    there.

4   **if** + *a modal verb,* + *a modal verb*
    If you **can't find** a cup, there **might be** one in the
    cupboard.
    Well, David **can't use** this kitchen **if** he **won't
    wash** up.

5   **if** + **will/would**, + *a modal verb*
    If you**'ll give** me your address, I **can send** you the
    information.
    If you **would** kindly **wait** a moment, please,
    Mr Barnes **won't be** long.

6   **if** + **should**, + *a modal verb/the imperative*
    I think it's going to be nice, but **if** it **should rain**,
    we **can have** the meal inside.
    I'll probably arrive on time, but **if** I **should be** late,
    please **don't wait** for me.

1   To give orders etc. ▷ 6.1
2   To talk about things that are always true.
3   Many uses, e.g. offering, giving advice.
4   Many uses, e.g. suggestions, permission.
5   To make a request. ▷ 31.2
6   To talk about future actions which the speaker
    thinks are not very probable.

For the three main types of if-clause ▷ 11.1. There
are many other types of if-clauses with different
verb tenses. These six types here are some of the
most usual ones.

12 Reported speech

12.1 Reporting verbs

1 Statements

Direct speech	'There's a game this evening.'
Reported speech	Peter **says** (**that**) there's a game this evening. There's a game this evening, Peter **says**.
Direct speech	'It begins at eight o'clock.'
Reported speech	Jane **told** me (**that**) it begins at eight o'clock. It begins at eight o'clock, Jane **told** me.

1 *say* and *tell* are reporting verbs which report statements or thoughts. We also use e.g. *mention, explain, answer, agree, write, think, know, be sure*. And ▷ 12.7

say does not have an indirect object when used as a reporting verb. *tell* must have an indirect object, e.g. *me*.

The reporting verb (e.g. *says*) usually comes before the reported clause (e.g. *there's a game this evening*), but the reported clause can come first. When the reporting verb comes first, we can use *that* or leave it out. Leaving it out is more informal.

When the reporting verb comes after the reported clause, we cannot use *that*.

2 Questions

Direct speech	'What time is the game?'
Reported speech	Andrew **asked** me what time the game was.

2 *ask* is a reporting verb which reports questions. We also use e.g. *wonder, enquire, want to know*.

▷ 12.6 reporting orders and requests; 39.3, 6 punctuation

12.2 Reporting in the present tense

Michael is reading Simon's letter and reporting what he reads to a friend.

'I'm having a great time in New York.'
Simon says he's having a great time in New York.

'My girl-friend likes it here, too.'
He mentions that his girl-friend likes it there, too.

'We'll be home next Tuesday.'
He says they'll be home tomorrow.

When the reporting verb is in the present tense (*says, mentions*), then the tense of the verb in direct speech (*'m having, likes, 'll be*) does not change.

Sometimes pronouns, adjectives and adverbs change in reported speech, e.g. *I →he, my →his, here →there, next Tuesday →tomorrow*.

We have to change these words when the situation has changed, e.g. New York is *here* for Simon but *there* for Michael because Michael is in England; the day when Simon comes home is *next Tuesday* for Simon but *tomorrow* for Michael because Michael reads the letter on Monday.

12.3 Reporting in the past tense [A]

Martin is reporting Barbara's words to Stephen.

1 'We **need** Stephen.'
Barbara said they **needed** you.

2 'I**'m starting** a pop group.'
She told me she **was starting** a pop group.

3 'I **haven't found** anyone who can play the guitar.'
She said she **hadn't found** anyone who could play the guitar.

4 'I**'ll be** at the club.'
She told me she**'d be** at the club.

5 'The group **is going to** meet there.'
She said that the group **was going to** meet there.

6 'I **must** talk to Stephen.'
She said she **had to** talk to you.

7 'He **played** in a group once.'
She mentioned that you **had played**/that you **played** in a group once.

8 'It **would** be great if he **could** play in our group.'
She said it **would** be great if you **could** play in their group.

If the reporting verb is in the past tense (e.g. *said, told*), then the verb in direct speech usually changes from the present to the past tense, e.g.

1 *need →needed*
2 *am →was*
3 *haven't →hadn't*
4 *will →would*
5 *is →was*
6 *must → had to*
7 If the verb in direct speech is in the past tense, it either changes to the past perfect tense (e.g. *played →had played*) or it stays the same.
8 *would, could, should, might* and *ought to* stay the same.

12.4   Reporting in the past tense [B]

Paul is reporting Sarah's words.

'Horses are my favourite animals.'
Sarah said horses **were** her favourite animals.
Sarah said horses **are** her favourite animals.

'I can ride.'
She told me she **could** ride.
She told me she **can** ride.

After a reporting verb in the past, there is usually a tense change. ▷ 12.3

But sometimes the verb in direct speech stays in the same tense if the words are still true when someone reports them, e.g. it is true that horses are still Sarah's favourite animals.

Even if the words are still true, *we can always change the tense* into the past after a past tense reporting verb.

12.5   Reporting questions

Mrs Todd is reporting a telephone conversation to her husband.

1 *Yes/no questions*

'Is your husband in?'
He asked **if** you were in.

'Has he gone to London?'
He wanted to know **whether** you'd gone to London.

2 *Wh-questions*

'Which train did he take?'
He asked me **which** train you'd taken.

'When does he usually get home?'
He asked **when** you usually got home.

1 We report yes/no questions with *if* or *whether*.
2 In wh-questions we use question words (e.g. *which, when, what, who* and *how*) both in direct speech and in reported speech.

Verbs in reported questions change in the same way as in reported statements. ▷ 12.3

The word order in a reported question is the same as in a direct statement (not a direct question), e.g. *you were in, you'd gone to London, you'd taken, you usually got home.*

12.6   Reporting orders and requests

1   'Take the pills before meals.'
The doctor **told me to** take the pills before meals.
'You mustn't smoke.'
He **told me not to** smoke.

2   'Would you mind not leaving your car here?'
Someone **asked me not to** leave the car there.

3   I **was told to** take the pills before meals.
You **were asked not to** leave the car there.

4   The doctor said I **must** take/I **had to** take/I **was to** take the pills before meals.
He said I **mustn't** smoke/I **was not to** smoke.

5   'Can I have some water please?'
A motorist **asked me for**/**asked for** some water.

6   He **asked if** he could have some water.

1   We report orders (▷ 31.1) with *tell* + object + infinitive.
2   We report requests (▷ 31.2) with *ask* + object + infinitive.
3   The reporting verb can be in the passive. ▷ 14.9
4   We can also report orders with a form of *must* or *be to*.
5   We report a request to have something with *ask for*.
6   We can also report requests which are in question form (e.g. *Can I . . .?*) in the same way as other yes/no questions. ▷ 12.5

12.7   Reporting suggestions, advice etc.

Suggestions	'Let's go out.' Tony **suggested going** out.	▷ 31.4
Advice	'You'd better phone the police.' Mrs Dell **advised** me **to phone** the police.	▷ 31.5
Warnings	'Don't be late.' I **warned** you **not to be** late.	▷ 31.7
Threats	'If you don't go, I'll call the police.' I **threatened to call** the police.	▷ 31.9
Insisting	'We simply must take a taxi.' Mr and Mrs Beal **insisted on taking** a taxi.	▷ 31.10
Refusals	'I'm not going to wait any longer.' Mrs Janner **refused to wait** any longer.	▷ 32.4
Promises	'I'll send you a postcard.' He **promised to send** us a postcard.	▷ 32.5
Offers	'Can I get you a taxi?' Eric **offered to get** the visitors a taxi.	▷ 33.1
Invitations	'Would you like to have lunch with us?' The Updikes **invited** us **to** lunch.	▷ 33.2

13 Tenses in sub clauses

13.1 Sequence of tenses

Why didn't you read what the notice **said**?
I thought he **was** an engineer.
We had already decided to buy the house
because we **liked** it so much.

If the main verb is in the past tense, then the verb
in a sub clause is often in a past tense too.

Even if the words are still true (the notice still says
something), we can use a past tense in the sub
clause.

▷ 12 reported speech

13.2 Sub clauses of future time

We'll start the meeting when everyone**'s** here.
If I **hear** any news, I'll phone you.
They're going to give a prize to the first person
who **finds** the answer.

If the main verb has a future meaning, then we use
the simple present tense in most sub clauses of
future time.

▷ 11 if-clauses

13.3 The unreal present and past

1   Just suppose we **had** enough money.
    (= but we haven't enough money)
    He acts as though he **was** the boss.
    (= but he isn't the boss)
    It's time we **went**.
    (= but we haven't gone yet)
2   I wish you**'d said** something.
    (= but you didn't say anything)
    I'd rather we **hadn't come**.
    (= but we have come)
    If we**'d booked** seats, we'd have been more
    comfortable.
    (= but we didn't book seats)

1   We use the past tense to talk about the unreal
    present.
2   We use the past perfect tense to talk about the
    unreal past.

    We can do this after certain words and phrases,
    e.g. *suppose, imagine, if, as if, as though, it's time,
    wish, if only, would rather.*

▷ 11 if-clauses; 30.8 having ideas; 34.5 wishing

14 The infinitive

14.1 The infinitive with **to** and without **to**

1a Are you ready **to go** now?
 b Don't forget we've a bus **to catch**.
 c I don't want **to be** late.
 d They expect us **to arrive** at seven.
 e Do you know where **to go**?
2a I must **finish** this homework.
 b Our English teacher makes us **work** very hard.
 c I'd better **do** it tonight, although I'd rather **go** out.

The infinitive is the base form of the verb, e.g. *go, catch, be*. We use it with *to* or without *to*.

1 The infinitive is with *to* after
a adjectives ▷ 14.2
b nouns ▷ 14.3
c verbs ▷ 14.4
d verb + object ▷ 14.5
e question words ▷ 14.11
2 The infinitive is without *to* after
a modal verbs ▷ 7.1
b *make/let/see/hear* + object ▷ 14.8; 16.3
c *had better* ▷ 31.5 and *would rather* ▷ 34.6

14.2 The infinitive after adjectives

1 I'm **glad to see** you all.
   The game was **exciting to watch.**
2 It would be more **interesting to go** out.
   The Top Club is the **easiest to find**.
3 This piano is **too heavy to move**.
   I'm not **strong enough to lift** it.
4 It's **good of you to come**.
   It was **silly of Peter not to tell** anyone.

1 The infinitive after an adjective is with *to*.
2 We can also use the comparative and superlative of adjectives (e.g. *more interesting, easiest*).
3 We can also use adjectives with *too* or *enough*.
4 We can use a phrase with *of* after adjectives like *good, kind, nice, helpful, silly, stupid, wrong*.

14.3 The infinitive after nouns and pronouns

Have you got **a book to read**?
(= a book you can read)
You'll need **something to eat**.
(= something you can eat)
I have **some letters to write**.
(= letters I must write)

The infinitive after a noun or pronoun is with *to*.

14.4 The infinitive after verbs

I've **decided to do** a course in nursing.
I **hope to get** a job near here.
I **want to find** somewhere to live.
I've **arranged to look** at a flat tomorrow.

For a list of verbs + infinitive with *to* and verbs + -ing form ▷ 16.1.

14.5 The infinitive after verb + object

Andy's father won't **allow him to use** the car.
I **persuaded my boss to pay** me more money.
No one **expected him to win**.
Jill's aunt **invited her to stay** for the weekend.

Some other verbs which can have an object and an infinitive with *to* are: *tell, ask* (▷ 12.6), *want* (▷ 14.6), *warn, advise, remind, teach, force.*

▷ 14.9 passive

14.6 **want someone to do something**

Do you **want me to cook** the dinner?
I**'d like you to help** if you can.

want and *would like* can have an object and an infinitive with *to*.
We cannot use a clause with *that* after *want* or *would like*.

14.7 Verb + infinitive with and without a noun phrase

We want to visit the Wilsons. (*We* visit the Wilsons.)
I expected to get a letter from them. (*I* get a letter.)
We want **the Wilsons** to visit us. (*The Wilsons* visit us.)
I expected **them** to write to us. (*They* write to us.)

We put a noun phrase (e.g. *the Wilsons, them*) before the infinitive when the subject of the sentence (*We* want, *I* expected) is not the same as the subject of the infinitive.

14.8   The infinitive without **to**: **make** and **let**

The government **forced** companies **to hold** down wage increases.
The government **made** companies **hold** down wage increases.
They **allowed** workers **to have** only a 5% increase.
They **let** workers **have** only a 5% increase.

The verbs *force* and *allow* +object have the infinitive with *to*. ▷ 14.5
The verbs *make* (= force) and *let* (= allow) + object have the infinitive without *to*.

▷   16.3 after *see, hear* etc.

14.9   The infinitive after the passive

The gunman forced the cashier to hand over the money.
The cashier **was forced to hand** over the money.
The teachers made everyone take the exam.
Everyone **was made to take** the exam.
The manager let Mr Jones leave early.
Mr Jones **was allowed to leave** early.

After the passive verb the infinitive is always with *to*.
We can also use these verbs in the passive: *tell, ask* (▷ 12.6), *warn, advise, teach, persuade, expect, invite*.
We do not use the verb *let* in the passive. We use *allow* instead.

14.10   **for** + noun phrase + infinitive

1   It was easy **for the player to kick** the ball into the empty goal.
(= The player easily kicked the ball into the empty goal.)
2   It was a mistake **for Helen to marry** Bob.
(= Helen married Bob, which was a mistake.)
3   We are still waiting **for them to reply**.
(= They have not replied yet.)

We use *for* + noun phrase + infinitive after
1   an adjective, e.g. *easy, important*
2   a noun phrase, e.g. *a mistake, a good idea*
3   a verb which usually has *for* after it, e.g. *wait for*

14.11 The infinitive after question words

I don't know **how to open** this bottle.
(= how I can open this bottle)

Can you tell me **where to buy** a ticket?
(= where I can buy a ticket)

Do you know **what to say**?
(= what you should say)

I've no idea **which bus to take**.
(= which bus I must take)

I can't decide **whether to go** or not.
(= whether I should go or not)

We can use the infinitive after question words and after *whether*.

14.12 Leaving out the verb after **to**

Did you look round the castle? ~
We wanted **to**, but we weren't allowed **to**.

We can leave out the verb after *to* if the meaning is clear without it.

14.13 Other forms of the infinitive

1 *Continuous infinitive*
   Those men seem **to be repairing** the road.
   They oughtn't **to be making** so much noise on a Sunday.

2 *Perfect infinitive*
   I should like **to have gone** for a walk, but it's been raining.
   We ought **to have spent** our holiday somewhere warmer.

3 *Passive infinitive*
   I'm going **to be interviewed** next week.
   I hope **to be offered** a job.

Form

1 *to be* + -ing form
   ▷ 7.14 modal verbs + *be* + -ing form

2 *to have* + -ed form (past participle)
   ▷ 7.15 modal verbs + *have* + -ed form

3 *to be* + -ed form (past participle)
   ▷ 10.5 modal verbs in the passive

15 The -ing form (verbal noun)

15.1 Introduction to the -ing form

1a **Smoking** isn't allowed here.
b I find **reading** difficult on a bus.
c This is a good place for **fishing**.
2 **Driving** a car isn't as comfortable as **travelling** by train.

1 We can use the -ing form as a verbal noun in the same way as we use other noun phrases. We can use it
a as a subject
b as an object
c after a preposition
2 After an -ing form we can put an object (e.g. *a car*) or an adverb phrase (e.g. *by train*).

▷ 31.1 orders

15.2 The -ing form after conjunctions and prepositions

1 **After working** all evening, John felt tired.
On hearing the news, they left at once.
We like a hot drink **before going** to bed.
I always have the radio on **while doing** the housework.
Judy hasn't found a job **since leaving** school.
Although feeling tired, David didn't want to stop.
In spite of trying so hard, I always make mistakes.
2 Can't you help **instead of** just **standing** there?
You won't pass the exam **without doing** any work.
You need a special tool **for cutting** glass.
Jane stayed awake **by drinking** black coffee.

The clause with the -ing form can come either before or after the main clause.
1 Using the -ing form to express time or contrast is a little formal. In speech we often use a clause with a subject, e.g. *after he'd worked all evening, as soon as they heard the news, before we go to bed*.
▷ 17.2; 27.2 clauses of time; 27.7 clauses of contrast
2 We use the -ing form after *instead of, without, for* and *by* even in informal speech.

▷ 27.9 clauses of purpose; 25.8 means; 31.4; 33.2 *What about/how about . . .?*

15.3 The -ing form after verbs

Have you **finished writing** the letter?
Barry **suggested going** for a walk.
I don't **mind waiting** a few minutes.
We **enjoy listening** to music.

For a list of verbs + -ing form and verbs + infinitive ▷ 16.1

15.4   The -ing form after **do**

Who's going to **do** the **cooking**?
You ought to **do** some **studying**.
I **did** a bit of **shopping** this morning.

We can use *do* with an -ing form to talk about a job of work, e.g. *cleaning, washing, ironing, typing.*

▷   17.5 the -ing form after *go*

15.5   The -ing form after verb/adjective + preposition

1   *Verb + preposition + -ing form*
I'm **thinking of buying** an electric toothbrush.
My brother's **talking about starting** a pop group.
We **succeeded in finding** the place.

2   *Adjective + preposition + -ing form*
Sarah's **fond of doing** crosswords.
You're **good at drawing**.
I'm a postman. I'm **used to walking**.

1   More examples of verb + preposition which can take an -ing form: *agree with, believe in, feel like, insist on, look forward to, take part in, worry about.*

▷   26.3 prepositional verbs

2   More examples of adjective + preposition which can take an -ing form: *afraid of, bored with, excited about, interested in, keen on, proud of, tired of.*

▷   25.12 adjective + preposition

15.6   The -ing form with a subject

1   We've stopped **watching** television.
(= We don't watch television any more.)
I insist on **having** a rest.
(= I insist that I have a rest.)

2   We've stopped **the children watching** television.
(= The children don't watch television any more.)
I insist on **you having** a rest, Sarah.
(= I insist that you have a rest.)

3   I insist on **your having** a rest.
I'm afraid of **Sarah's doing** too much.

1   When the subject of the sentence (*We*'ve stopped, *I* insist) is the same as the subject of the -ing form, we do not repeat the subject before the -ing form.

2   When the subject of the sentence is *not* the same as the subject of the -ing form (*The children* don't watch television, *You* have a rest), then we give the -ing form its own subject, too.

3   The subject of the -ing form can be a possessive form (e.g. *your, Sarah's*), but usually only if it is a pronoun or a name. A possessive form is more formal than e.g. *you, Sarah.*

15.7   The passive -ing form

Visiting people is nicer than **being visited**.
He was afraid of **being seen** by the police.
I don't like the dog **being shut** up in the house.

Form *being* + -ed form (past participle)

16 The infinitive and the -ing form

16.1 The infinitive and the -ing form after verbs

I **wanted to visit** England.
I **enjoy travelling** around.

After some verbs we use the infinitive with *to*
(▷ 14.4), and after some verbs we use the -ing
form (▷ 15.3).
Here are some of the most common verbs of both types.

+ *the infinitive with* **to**			+ *the -ing form*	
agree	fail	plan	avoid	miss
arrange	forget ▷ 16.2	prepare	can't help	practise
attempt	have ▷ 7.4	promise	dislike	risk
be ▷ 4.8	hope	refuse	enjoy	stop ▷ 16.2
can afford	learn	seem	finish	suggest
choose	manage	used ▷ 3.11	go on	*And*
dare ▷7.13	need ▷ 7.4	want	imagine	it's no fun
decide	offer	wish	keep	it's no good
expect	ought ▷ 7.6		mind	it's no use
				it's worth

16.2 The infinitive and the -ing form: special cases

1   Mrs Scott **began to eat/began eating** her dinner.
    She **intended to go/intended going** out later.

2   I **like to have/like having** tea in front of the
    television.
    I **love to read/love reading** at meal times.

3   I **like to go** to the doctor every year.
    I **like to know** if there's anything wrong with me.

4   Dick **would like to stay** in, but I'd prefer to sit
    outside.

1   After *begin, start, continue* and *intend*, we use
    either the infinitive or the -ing form.

2   After *like, love, prefer* and *hate*, we use either the
    infinitive or the -ing form. ▷ 34.3 likes; 34.6
    preferences. But see the special use in 3.

3   We use an infinitive after *like* to talk about
    something a person chooses to do but may not
    enjoy doing.

4   After *would like* (= want), *would love, would prefer*
    and *would hate*, we use the infinitive.
    ▷ 34.5 wishes; 34.6 preferences

5 He **remembered to bring** the drinks.
He **didn't forget to bring** the drinks.

6 I **remember having** a picnic here years ago.
I'**ll never forget having** a picnic here years ago.

7 I'**m trying to get** brown in the sun.

8 Why don't you **try putting** some cream on your back?

9 I **stopped to get** some aspirin as I was driving from the hotel.

10 Your tooth will **stop hurting** if you take two of these.

5 We use an infinitive after *remember* or *not forget* when we remember that we have to do something.

6 We use an -ing form after *remember* or *not forget* when we remember something that happened in the past.

7 We use an infinitive after *try* when *try* means to make an attempt, to do your best to succeed.

8 We use an -ing form after *try* when *try* means to make an experiment, to do something as a test to see if it will succeed.

9 We use an infinitive after *stop* when someone stops in order to do something. ▷ 27.9 clauses of purpose

10 We use an -ing form after *stop* to talk about something finishing, something that no longer happens.

16.3 The infinitive without **to** and the -ing form after **see, hear** etc.

1 We saw a group of people. They climbed the hill.
We saw a group of people **climb** the hill.
(= We saw them do the whole climb to the top.)

We heard a man. He shouted.
We heard a man **shout**.
(= He shouted once, and we heard the shout.)

2 We saw a group of people. They were climbing the hill.
We saw a group of people **climbing** the hill.
(= But we did not see them do the whole climb.)

We heard a man. He was shouting.
We heard a man **shouting**.
(= He shouted a number of times, and we heard some of the shouts.)

1 We use the infinitive without *to* after verbs of perception (*see, hear* etc.) and with *watch* and *listen to* to talk about a complete action.

2 We use the -ing form after these verbs to talk about part of an action, but not the whole action from beginning to end.

17 The -ing form and the -ed form (participles)

17.1 The -ing form and the -ed form used as adjectives

1 The men ran out to the **waiting** car.
There were three people inside the **burning** house.

2 The **injured** man was taken to hospital.
The **stolen** money was in **used** notes.
She tried to open the door, but it was **locked**.

1 The -ing form (present participle) describes an action (the car was waiting).

2 The -ed form (past participle) describes the result of an action (something had injured the man).

For e.g. *the car waiting outside* ▷ 22.11
For the -ed form in the passive ▷ 10.1, 2

17.2 The -ing form in clauses of time

1 Jane ate her supper while she was sitting in front of the television.
She heard the telephone and got up to answer it.

2 Jane ate her supper **while sitting** in front of the television.
On hearing the telephone, she got up to answer it.

3a **Sitting** in front of the television, Jane ate her supper.

b **Hearing** the telephone, she got up to answer it.

c Jane ate her supper **sitting** in front of the television.

1 To talk about two actions that happen at the same time or that happen one after the other, we can use two clauses.

2 We can replace one of the clauses by an -ing form after a conjunction or preposition. ▷ 15.2

3a We can use an -ing form without a conjunction or preposition to talk about an action that happens at the same time as another action.

b We can also use an -ing form without a conjunction or preposition to talk about an action that happens just before another action. The -ing form comes before the main clause.

c If the actions happen at the same time, the -ing form can come after the main clause.

An -ing form before the main clause is rather formal, and we normally use it only in writing.

17.3 The perfect -ing form in clauses of time

Compare the use of the past perfect and the -ing form:

1 After she had counted the money, she locked it in a drawer.
2 **After counting** the money, she locked it in a drawer.
3 **Having counted** the money, she locked it in a drawer.

Form *having* + -ed form

Use

1 Remember that we use the past perfect tense to talk about the first of two actions in the past. ▷ 3.6
2 We can use *after* + -ing form in the same way. ▷ 15.2
3 We can also use the perfect -ing form without *after* to talk about the first of two actions in the past.

The sentences with -ing forms are used much more in writing than in speech.

17.4 The -ing form and the -ed form in clauses of reason

1a They didn't know the way, so they soon got lost.
 b Not **knowing** the way, they soon got lost.
2a The plane was delayed by bad weather, so it took off three hours late.
 b **Delayed** by bad weather, the plane took off three hours late.
3a I had got up early, so I felt pretty tired.
 b **Having got up** early, I felt pretty tired.

We can use the -ing form and the -ed form to give a reason. We can use these forms:

1b the -ing form
2b the -ed form (which has a passive meaning)
3b the perfect -ing form ▷ 17.3

We use the -ing form and the -ed form to give a reason more often in writing than in speech.

17.5 The -ing form after **go**

We **go dancing** every weekend.
The boys **went swimming** yesterday.
Are you **going sailing** again soon?

We can use *go* + -ing form to talk about things we go out to do, especially in our free time, e.g. *walking, climbing, fishing, riding, skating, shopping.*

▷ 15.4 the -ing form after *do*

18 Nouns

18.1 Regular plurals of nouns

my coat	our coat**s**	a bus	three bus**es**
a book	book**s**	a dish	some dish**es**
a dog	some dog**s**		
one day	two day**s**		

The regular plural ending is *-s/-es*.
We use *-es* after [s], [z], [ʃ] etc. ▷ 38.2

▷ 38.1 pronunciation

18.2 Irregular plurals of nouns

1 a potato — some potato**es**
  a tomato — a pound of tomato**es**

2 a pony — a lot of pon**ies**
  the factory — both factor**ies**

3 a knife — the kni**ves** [vz]
  the shelf — the shel**ves** [vz]

4 his mouth — their mouths [ðz]
  a path — two paths [ðz]

5 a house — a lot of houses [zɪz]

6 her child [tʃaɪld] — her child**ren** [ˈtʃɪldrən]
  an ox — two ox**en**

7 a sheep — some sheep
  an aircraft — two aircraft

8 a foot — six feet [fiːt]
  a tooth — teeth [tiːθ]
  the goose — the geese [giːs]
  a mouse — some mice [maɪs]
  the woman — the women [ˈwɪmɪn]
  a man — two men [men]
  a policeman — three policemen [mən]
  (+ postmen, milkmen etc.)

9 one penny — ten pence/ten pennies
  a person — people/persons
  a fish — a lot of fish/three fishes

1 We add *-es* after *o* in *potato, tomato, hero*. But *photo, piano, radio* have *-s* (*photos, pianos, radios*).

2 After a consonant, *y* changes to *ies* in the plural ▷ 38.6, but when *y* comes after a vowel, the plural is regular, e.g. *keys, boys, ways*.

3 *f* and *fe* change to *ves* in *knife, shelf, wolf, thief, calf, half, wife, life, leaf, loaf*. But *chief, cliff* and *roof* are regular (*chiefs, cliffs, roofs*).

4 [θ] becomes [ðz] in *mouth, path, bath, youth*. But *birth, death* and *month* are regular [θs].

5 *house* [s] becomes *houses* [zɪz].

6 *child* and *ox* have plurals in *-ren, -en*.

7 *sheep, deer*, most names of fish (e.g. *salmon, trout*) and *aircraft, spacecraft* and *hovercraft* have the same singular and plural forms.

8 In some words the vowel changes and there is no *-s*.

9 *ten pence* is an amount of money ▷ 36.10; *ten pennies* means ten penny coins. *people* is the normal plural; *persons* is formal. *fish* is the normal plural; *fishes* is less usual. *three fishes* can mean three different kinds of fish.

▷ 18.12 pair nouns; 18.13 nouns with a plural form; 23.10 nationality words

18.3 Direct and indirect objects

What did Debbie give her mother/her father?

1a Debbie gave **her mother a scarf** for Christmas.
 b She gave **her a scarf**.
2a She bought **her father some cigars**.
 b She bought **him some cigars**.

Who did she give the scarf/the cigars to?

3a She gave **the scarf to her mother**.
 b She gave **it to her mother**.
 c She gave **it to her**.
4a She bought **the cigars for her father**.
 b She bought **them for her father**.
 c She bought **them for him**.

1,2 The indirect object without *to* or *for* comes before the direct object.

3,4 The indirect object with *to* or *for* comes after the direct object.

3 We use *to* with *give, hand, lend, offer, owe, pass, pay, promise, read, sell, send, show, take, teach, tell* and *write*.

4 We use *for* with *buy, cook, fetch, find, get, leave, make, order, reserve* and *save*.
 With *bring* we can use *to* or *for*.

We can use a pronoun
1b,2b instead of an indirect object
3b,4b instead of a direct object
3c,4c instead of both an indirect and a direct object

▷ 10.6 passive

18.4 The possessive form of nouns

1 *Singular nouns*
 That's my brother**'s** watch.
 Whose chair is that? ~ It's Ben**'s**.

2 *Plural nouns*
 Is that a girl**s'** school or a boy**s'** school?
 The Atkinson**s'** house is for sale.

3 *Irregular plural nouns without* **-s/-es**
 The men**'s** toilets are over there.
 There's a children**'s** playground in the park.

Form

1 With singular nouns we use an apostrophe + *s*.
2 With plural nouns we put an apostrophe after the *s*.
3 With irregular plural nouns that do not end in *-s/-es* we use an apostrophe + *s*.

We can leave out the noun if the meaning is clear without it, e.g. *It's Ben's* = It's Ben's chair.

Use

We use the possessive form with persons to show that something *belongs* to somebody or that something is *for* somebody (*a girls' school* = a school *for* girls). But ▷ 18.5–7

▷ 38.1 pronunciation; 38.6 with *-y*

18.5 The possessive form in phrases of place

Have you been to the chemist**'s**?
I've been at the Wilson**s'** all afternoon.

the chemist's = the chemist's shop
the Wilsons' = the Wilsons' house/the Wilson family's house

18.6 The possessive form in phrases of time

I read about the strike in **yesterday's** paper.
The workers have lost a **week's** wages.
They want five **weeks'** holiday.
It's a 15 **minutes'** drive to the factory.

yesterday's paper =	the paper that came out yesterday
a week's wages =	wages for a week
five weeks' holiday =	a holiday that lasts five weeks
a 15 minutes' drive =	a distance that we can drive in 15 minutes

For *15-minute drive* ▷ 37.7

18.7 **of** used instead of the possessive form

1 *With things*
There were people picnicking on **the bank of the river**.
It was **the beginning of the holidays**.

2 *With people*
We could hear **the voices of children** playing in the water.
I walked in **the footprints of the man** in front of me.

1 We normally use *of* instead of the possessive form (▷ 18.4) before the name of a *thing*. We use it to show that something (e.g. *the bank*) belongs to or is part of another thing (e.g. *the river*).

2 We also use *of* instead of the possessive form with *people* when the noun has a phrase or clause after it which describes the noun, e.g. *children* playing in the water.

For *the river bank* ▷ 37.2

18.8   Countable and uncountable nouns

1   *Countable nouns*
a   We need **a teapot** and **some cups**. We don't need **spoons**.
b   Here's **the teapot**, and here are **our cups**.
c   There are **two cups**.

2   *Uncountable nouns*
a   We need **some milk** and **some tea**. I don't take **sugar**.
b   Here's **the milk**, and here's **our tea**.
c   There are **two bottles of milk**.

1   *teapot, cup* and *spoon* are countable nouns. Countable nouns have a plural form, e.g. *cups*. We can say
a   *a cup, some cups, cups*
b   *the cup, the cups; my cup, our cups* etc.
c   *two cups, three cups* etc.

2   *milk, tea* and *sugar* are uncountable nouns. Uncountable nouns do *not* have a plural form (but ▷ 18.10). We can say
a   *some milk, milk*
b   *the milk; my milk, your milk* etc.
c   We cannot use a number + uncountable noun. To say *how much* milk, we use a countable noun + *of* e.g. *two bottles of milk*. ▷ 18.9

▷   19.2 *a/an, the*; 20.17 *a lot of, many, much*

18.9   Countable and uncountable nouns: **of** in phrases of quantity

1   *Countable nouns*
a box **of** matches
two packets **of** cigarettes
a kilo **of** apples
six pounds **of** potatoes

2   *Uncountable nouns*
a bottle **of** milk
two tins **of** meat
half a pound **of** tea
five litres **of** oil
a drop **of** water
two pieces **of** paper
a bar **of** chocolate
six loaves **of** bread

We use a noun (e.g. *box, packets*) + *of*
1   with a countable noun when it is easier to say how many e.g. boxes or kilos than to say how many e.g. matches or apples
2   with an uncountable noun (e.g. *milk, meat*) whenever we need to say how much milk or meat

▷   20.22 quantifiers + *of*

18.10   Uncountable nouns made countable

1   Two cups of tea and one cup of coffee, please. **Two teas** and **one coffee**, please.
2   We had different kinds of wine and cheese. We had different **wines** and **cheeses**.

1   We sometimes use uncountable nouns as countable nouns when we are ordering drinks or food.
2   We can also use uncountable nouns as countable nouns when we are talking about *a kind of* or *kinds of* wine, cheese, fruit, wool etc.

18.11 Uncountable nouns: **information, news, advice, work** etc.

1 I've got **some information**.
Steven's heard **some** exciting **news**.
Can I give you **some advice**?

2 I've got two **pieces of information**.
Steven's heard an exciting **bit of news**.
Can I give you a **piece of advice**?

3 We've got **work** to do.
We've got **a job** to do.

1 *information, news* and *advice* are uncountable nouns. Note the following words, which are also uncountable:
furniture, luggage, progress, research, weather, work, homework, housework, travel, money.

2 To make these noun phrases countable, we can use *piece* or *bit + of.*

3 Sometimes there is a countable noun with a similar meaning, e.g. *work/a job, travel/a journey, money/a coin* or *a note.*

18.12 Pair nouns

1 I need **some trousers**.
My **glasses are** broken.
These tights are expensive.

2 I need **a pair of trousers**.
Luckily I've got **two pairs of glasses**.

1 Pair nouns (e.g. *trousers, glasses*) are always plural in form.

2 If we want to say how many, we use *pair(s) of.*

Other pair nouns: *pyjamas, shorts, pants, jeans, spectacles, binoculars, scissors, pliers, scales.*

18.13 Other nouns with a plural form

1 *With a plural verb*
His clothes were old and dirty.
The goods are still at the docks.

2 *With a singular verb*
Mathematics is a difficult subject.
The news is at ten o'clock on ITV.

3 *With a plural or a singular verb*
The company's **headquarters is/are** in Leeds.
The cheapest **means** of transport **is** the bicycle/**are** the bicycle and the motorcycle.

Here are some other nouns that have a plural form but no singular form:

1 with a plural verb: *riches, thanks, contents, troops, earnings, savings*

2 with a singular verb: *measles, politics, athletics, gymnastics*

3 with a plural or a singular verb: *works* (= factory)

18.14 Collective nouns

1 **The family has** lived here for hundreds of years.
The government isn't very popular.

2 **The family have** all gone on holiday.
Manchester United aren't playing very well.

3 **The police are** questioning two men.

1 We use the singular form of the verb after a collective noun (e.g. *family*) if we are thinking of the group as a whole.

2 We use a plural verb if we are thinking of the group as a number of individual people.

3 The verb is always plural after *police* and *cattle*.
Other collective nouns: *group, gang, club, team, crowd, audience, public, class, committee, army, company; Liverpool, the BBC, Esso* and other names of sports teams, organizations and companies.

18.15 Noun phrases of measurement

Five hundred miles is a long way.
£35 seems a lot of money for a shirt.

We use the singular form of the verb after a noun phrase of measurement or amount.

18.16 Apposition

1 **The playwright William Shakespeare** was born at Stratford.

2 He was born at **Stratford, a small town in the English Midlands**.

3 It was a special day yesterday for **14-year-old schoolboy Mark Jones**.

We can use two noun phrases one after the other to refer to the same thing. The phrases are in apposition.

1 When the second phrase defines the meaning of the first (e.g. tells us *which* playwright), we do not use a comma.

2 When the second phrase adds extra information about the first but does not define it, we use a comma.

3 *the* is often left out of the first phrase, especially in newspaper reports.

19 The articles: *a/an* and *the*

19.1 The pronunciation of the articles

a/an		the	
a song	[ə] + [s]	**the** song	[ðə] + [s]
a new bed	[ə] + [n]	**the** new bed	[ðə] + [n]
a union	[ə] + [j]	**the** union	[ðə] + [j]
an apple	[ən] + [æ]	**the** apple	[ðɪ] + [æ]
an old tin	[ən] + [əʊ]	**the** old tin	[ðɪ] + [əʊ]
an hour	[ən] + [aʊ]	**the** hour	[ðɪ] + [aʊ]

We use *a* [ə] before a consonant sound and *an* [ən] before a vowel sound.

We use *the* [ðə] before a consonant sound and *the* [ðɪ] before a vowel sound.

19.2 **a/an** and **the**

1 There's **a man** and some girls in the water.

2a **The man** is swimming, but **the girls** aren't.

b **The sun** is shining.

c **The beach** is empty now.
The water is nice and warm.

3 There's **a hotel** in the High Street where you can stay.
There's only **one hotel** in this town.

1 We use *a/an* only with singular countable nouns. In the plural we use *some*. ▷ 19.3
a/an = one. *a man* = one man (but we don't know *which* man), a man not mentioned before.

2 We use *the* with countable nouns (singular and plural) and with uncountable nouns.
We use *the*

a before nouns already mentioned. *The man* = the man I have just spoken about

b before e.g. *sun* because there is only one sun

c when it is clear that the speaker is talking about one special thing. *The beach* = this beach I am talking about (we know which beach).

3 We use *one*, not *a/an*, when we are interested in number, e.g. one hotel, not two or three.

19.3   **a/an** and **some**

Singular nouns

1a   Look, there's **a horse** in the field.
b   It's **a pony**, not a horse.
c   **A horse** is bigger than a pony.

Plural nouns

2a   I'm going to buy **some apples**.
b   No, let's get **oranges** today.
c   Well, **apples** are cheaper at the moment.

Uncountable nouns

3a   Would you like **some tea**?
b   Is this **tea** or coffee?
c   I like **tea** best.

1a   We use *a/an* only with singular countable nouns. *a/an* means *one*. ▷ 19.2
b   We use *a/an* when we are talking about what something is, e.g. *a pony*, not a horse.
c   We also use e.g. *a horse* to talk about all horses.
2a   With plural nouns we use *some. some apples* = a number of apples.
b   We use a plural noun without *some* when we are talking about e.g. *oranges* (and not apples), and we are not interested in how many oranges.
c   We also use a plural noun without *some* to talk about e.g. all apples.
3a   We can also use *some* with uncountable nouns.
b   We use an uncountable noun without *some* when we are talking about e.g. *tea* (and not coffee); and we are not interested in how much tea.
c   We also use an uncountable noun without *some* to talk about e.g. all tea.

▷   18.8 countable and uncountable nouns; 20.14 *some* and *any*

19.4   **a/an** before jobs, nationalities and beliefs

1   Mr Malone is **a** writer and Mrs Stein is **an** artist.
2a   He's **an** Englishman and she's **an** American.
b   He's English and she's American.
3   He's **a** Catholic and she's **a** Protestant.

1   We use *a/an* before a noun saying what a person's job is. We cannot leave out *a/an*.
2a   We use *a/an* before a noun of nationality.
b   We can also use an adjective to give a person's nationality. ▷ 23.10
3   We use *a/an* before nouns which say what a person believes in.

19.5   **a/an** with **quite, such** and **rather**

1   The party was quite good.
    We had **quite a good** time.
    The story was so funny.
    It was **such a funny** story.

2   The picture is rather nice.
    It's **rather a nice** picture./**a rather nice** picture.

1   We can use *quite* and *such* before *a/an* but not after it.

2   We can use *rather* either before or after *a/an*. The meaning is the same.

▷   24.8 adverbs of degree

19.6   **a/an** in phrases of price, speed etc.

These apples are forty pence **a** kilo.
You can only do thirty miles **an** hour on this road.

In these phrases *a/an* means *each* or *every*.

▷   24.7 frequency

19.7   Uncountable nouns with and without **the**

1   **Meat** is expensive.
    Crime is increasing.
    We can learn a lot from **history**.

2   **The meat at our supermarket** costs a lot.
    The crime we read about in the papers is terrible.
    This book is about **the history of Europe**.

1   We do not use *the* before an uncountable noun with a general meaning. *Meat* = all meat.

2   But we use *the* before an uncountable noun with a limited meaning, e.g. *the meat at our supermarket*.

19.8   **school, prison** etc. with and without **the**

1   **School** is over at four o'clock.
    The man was sent to **prison** for stealing cars.
    Mrs Lee is in **hospital**. She's very ill.

2   **The school** cost a lot of money to build.
    The visitors came out of **the prison**.
    She's in **the** new **hospital**.

3   Judy's gone to **work**.
    She's gone to **the office**.

We sometimes leave out *the* before *school, prison, hospital, work, church, college, university, class, court, market, town, home, bed* and *sea*.

1   We leave out *the* when we are talking about school, prison etc. as an institution, and we are interested in what we use it for.

2   But we use *the* if we are talking about a school, prison etc. as a building. We must use *the* if there is a word or phrase describing the noun, e.g. *the new hospital*.

3   We leave out *the* before *work* (= place of work), but we use *the* before *office, factory* and *shop*.

19.9   Phrases of time without **the**

Years	in **1978**; after **1984**	But	in **the** year 1978
Seasons	**Winter** begins next week. It's nice here in **summer**.	Or	It's nice here in **the** summer.
Months	since **May**; **January** is often cold.	But	**The** January of 1979 was very cold.
Special times of the year	**Easter** is in April this year. Are you going away at **Christmas**?	But	Do you remember **the** first Christmas we spent together?
Days	on **Tuesday**; before **Friday**	But	on **the** Tuesday before last
Parts of the day and night	at **midday**; at **night**	But	in **the** morning; during **the** afternoon; in **the** evening; in **the** night
Meals	We had eggs for **breakfast**. **Dinner** is at half past seven.	But	I didn't like **the** breakfast we had this morning.

▷   25.3 prepositions of time; 25.9 *by*

19.10   Names with and without **the**

1	*People*	This is **Mrs Orton**. **David**'s here.	But	**the** Lawsons(= the Lawson family)
2	*Continents*	Have you been to **Africa**?		
3	*Countries*	**England** is a small country. I come from **Canada**.	But	**the** West Indies from **the** United States to **the** Netherlands in **the** USSR
4	*Lakes and mountains*	Chicago is on **Lake Michigan**. Who first climbed **Mount Everest**?	But	in **the** Highlands **the** Alps
5	*Rivers, canals and seas*			on **the** River Thames through **the** Suez Canal in **the** Atlantic Ocean

6   *Cities, towns*   We stayed in **New York**.
    and villages

But   in **the** Hague

7   *Streets, parks*   in **Oxford Street**
    and bridges   near **Piccadilly Circus**
                      through **Hyde Park**
                      Tower Bridge

But   in **the** High Street
      the Strand, **the** Mall
      the Oxford road (= the road to Oxford)
      the Severn Bridge (= the bridge over
      the River Severn)

8   *Theatres, cinemas, hotels,*
    museums and galleries

      the Shakespeare (Theatre)
      at **the** Classic (Cinema)
      the Hilton (Hotel)
      near **the** British Museum
      in **the** National Gallery
      the Empire State Building

9   *Other buildings*   to **Buckingham Palace**
                        outside **Westminster Abbey**
                        at **Shell-Mex House**
                        near **Victoria Station**
                        from **Heathrow Airport**

But   at **the** White House

10   *Phrases with* **of**
                    But   at London University

      in **the** House of Commons
      at **the** University of London
      the England of Shakespeare

We do not use *the* before the names of
1   people
2   continents
3   countries
4   lakes and mountains
6   cities, towns and villages
7   streets, parks and bridges
9   buildings other than hotels, museums etc.

We use *the* before
1   plural names referring to a whole family ▷ 18.5
3,4   plural place names and e.g. *USSR, UK*
5   the names of rivers, canals and seas
8   the names of theatres, cinemas, hotels, museums
    and galleries
10   phrases with *of*

20 Pronouns and quantifiers

20.1 Personal pronouns

Subject forms

1 **I**'ve got three bags.
2 **You** need some money.
3 What about Philip? Where is **he**?
4 Where's Jane? Is **she** coming?
5 What about the taxi? Where is **it**?
6 **We**'re late.
7 Where are the others? Are **they** coming?

Object forms

Help **me** with the bags, please.
I'll give **you** £5.
We're waiting for **him**.
This is **her** now.
I can't see **it**.
Can you take **us** with you?
Tell **them** to come now.

Form

	Singular		Plural	
	Subject	Object	Subject	Object
1st person	**I**	**me**	**we**	**us**
2nd person	**you**	**you**	**you**	**you**
3rd person	**he**	**him**	**they**	**them**
	she	**her**		
	it	**it**		

Use

We use pronouns to talk about the speaker (*I, we*) or the person we are speaking to (*you*). We also use them instead of a noun phrase when there is no need to say the full phrase (*he, she, it, they*).

We use the object form when the pronoun is

1 the direct object
2 the indirect object ▷ 18.3
3 after a preposition
4 the complement of the verb *be*

We use

1 *I/me* for the speaker
2 *you* for the person or the people spoken to
3 *he/him* to talk about a boy or man or a male animal, especially a pet animal
4 *she/her* to talk about a girl or woman or a female animal, especially a pet animal
5 *it* for a thing or an animal. And ▷ 20.2, 3
6 *we/us* for the speaker and another person or people
7 *they/them* for people or things. And ▷ 20.3, 4

20.2 Uses of **it**

1a	Where's my watch? Have you seen **it**?		1a	to talk about a thing (e.g. *my watch*)
b	There's someone at the door. ~ **It**'s Bob.		b	to talk about a person when we are saying or asking who the person is. *It* = the person at the door.
2	**It**'s getting late and **it**'s still raining.		2	as subject in sentences about time or the weather
3	**It** seems that no one is coming.		3	as subject before *seem, appear* and *happen*
4a	**It** would be silly to go out now. (= To go out now would be silly.)		4	as subject when the subject clause (e.g. *to go out now, that they haven't telephoned*) comes later in the sentence
b	**It**'s strange that they haven't telephoned. (= That they haven't telephoned is strange.)			
5	**It** was Pamela who wanted to go sailing. (= *Pamela* wanted to go sailing.)		5	to emphasize a word or phrase, e.g. *Pamela* ▷ 28.4

We use *it*

▷ 5.3 *it/there + be*; 10.9 *it + passive verb + clause*

20.3 **it, one, them** and **some**

1a	I've got the camera. **It**'s here.		1a	*the, this, my* etc. + singular noun →*it*
b	I must buy a film. I'll get **one** today.		b	*a/an* + singular noun →*one*
2a	Have you seen these stamps? I like **them** better than the usual ones.		2a	*the, these, my* etc. + plural noun →*they/them*
b	I need some stamps. I want **some** for these letters.		b	*some* + plural noun →*some*
3a	The coffee's nice. Where did you get **it**?		3a	*the, this, my* etc. + uncountable noun → *it*
b	We need some coffee. I'll get **some** today.		b	*some* + uncountable noun →*some*

▷ 19.3 *a/an* and *some*; 20.21 quantifiers without a noun

20.4 A special use of **you, one, they** and **people**

1	**You** can't do much without money.		1	We sometimes use *you* to talk about people in general (= everyone), including the speaker.
2	**One** can't do much without money.		2	We also use *one* to talk about people in general, including the speaker. *one* is more formal than *you*.
3a	**They**'re building a new office block.		3a	We sometimes use *they* to talk about a group of people if it is not important to say who they are.
b	**They** ought to do something about all this pollution.		b	We sometimes use *they* to talk about the government or people in authority.
c	**They** say he's a good doctor.		c	We use *they* for other people in general.
4	**People** say he's a good doctor.		4	We use *people* for other people in general.

20.5   Possessive adjectives and pronouns

Possessive adjectives
That isn't **my** key.
Put **your** hands in **your** pockets.
Here's Jim's coat. Give him **his** coat.
Mary wants **her** bag.
The house lost **its** roof in the storm.
Can we have **our** records?
Where's the Arnolds' car? They can't find **their** car.

Form

my key	**mine**	**our** records	**ours**
your hands	**yours**		
his coat	**his**	**their** car	**theirs**
her hat	**hers**		
its roof			

We use possessive adjectives with a noun and possessive pronouns without a noun.

Possessive pronouns
Mine's here.
My hands are warm, but **yours** are cold.
It isn't **his**. It's Bill's.
This is **hers**.

We want **ours**, too.
Theirs is a blue Mini. That green car is the Grays'.

Use

We use possessive adjectives and pronouns to show that something belongs to somebody.

We use possessive adjectives and pronouns with parts of the body (e.g. *your hands*) and clothes (e.g. *your pockets*).

Note *its* is a possessive adjective. *it's* = it is.

▷   18.4 possessive form

20.6   Possessive adjective + **own**

Ben's got **his own** room now. He doesn't share with Dick any more.
Why don't you buy **your own** newspaper?

my own room = the room that belongs to me and not to anyone else

▷   20.11 *on my own*

20.7   **of** + possessive pronoun

Laura is a friend **of mine**.
I've got some records **of hers**.

a friend of mine = one of my friends

20.8   Reflexive pronouns

I'm teaching **myself** Italian.
Are you enjoying **yourself**?
Ernest Hemingway killed **himself**.
My sister can look after **herself**.
This kettle switches **itself** off.
We've found **ourselves** a nice place here.
Can you all help **yourselves** to sandwiches?
The children are behaving **themselves** today.

Form

myself	**ourselves**
yourself	**yourselves**
himself	**themselves**
herself	
itself	

The singular pronouns end in -*self*, e.g. *yourself*.
The plural pronouns end in -*selves*, e.g.
yourselves.

Use

We use a reflexive pronoun to talk about the same person or thing that we mentioned in the subject of the sentence.

Note *enjoy yourself* = have a good time
help yourself to sandwiches = take some sandwiches
behave yourself = not be silly or naughty

20.9   Emphatic pronouns

We decorated this room **ourselves**.
The Queen **herself** visited the town last year.
I'll do it **myself**.

Form

The emphatic pronouns have the same form as the reflexive pronouns. ▷ 20.8

The emphatic pronoun has end position (*We . . . ourselves*), or it comes after the noun phrase it refers to (*The Queen herself . . .*).

Use

We use an emphatic pronoun to lay emphasis on a noun phrase, e.g. *we, the Queen. we ourselves* = we and no one else.

▷   20.11 *by myself*

20.10 **themselves** and **each other**

Both boys hurt **themselves** when they fell.
(= Each boy hurt himself.)
The two boxers hurt **each other**.
(= Each boxer hurt the other.)

20.11 **on my own** and **by myself**

The old man lives **on his own/by himself**.
I don't want to go out **on my own/by myself**.

on my own/by myself = alone, without anyone else

20.12 Demonstrative adjectives and pronouns

Demonstrative adjectives
What about **this** tie here?
I like **that** dress there.
These shirts are nice, look.
Those coats are expensive.

Demonstrative pronouns
This is a nice colour.
That's cheap.
These are my size.
Do you like **those** over there?

Form

this	that
these	those

this and *that* are singular; *these* and *those* are plural.
For *this one* ▷ 20.13

Use

We use *this* and *these* to talk about things near the speaker.
We use *that* and *those* to talk about things that are further away from the speaker.

20.13 one and ones

1 *After an adjective*
   Do you want a big bottle or a **small one**? The **big ones** cost £1.50.

2 *After the*
   Our house is **the one** on the corner.
   I don't like these plates as much as **the ones** we first looked at.

3 *After every*
   We've seen plenty of coats. You've looked at **every one** in the shop.

4 *After each*
   We've sixty tickets. **Each (one)** has a number.

5 *After a demonstrative adjective*
   Which card do you want, **this (one)** or **that (one)**?
   These (ones) are nicer than **those (ones)**.

6 *After which*
   You've seen all the suits. **Which (one)** do you want?
   You've seen all the shoes. **Which (ones)** do you want?

7 **one** *replacing a noun phrase*
   We've got some biscuits. Would you like **one**?

We use *one* instead of a singular noun (a small bottle → a small one).
We use *ones* instead of a plural noun (the big bottles → the big ones).

We use *one/ones*

1 after an adjective in a noun phrase
2 after *the*
3 after *every* ▷ 20.15

   We can use *one/ones* (but we can leave it out)

4 after *each* ▷ 20.15
5 after a demonstrative adjective, especially after *this* and *that* ▷ 20.12
6 after *which* ▷ 21.3

7 We can use *one* instead of a noun phrase with *a/an* (a biscuit →one). ▷ 20.3

20.14 some and any

1 I've got **some** money.
   There are **some** oranges at the shop.

2 I haven't got **any** food.
   Have you got **any** water?
   There aren't **any** apples at the shop.
   Are there **any** bananas?

3 Would you like **some** water? ~ Yes, please.
   Can I have **some** bananas, please?

1 We use *some* in positive sentences.
2 We use *any* in negative sentences and in questions. But ▷ 20.15
3 We use *some* in questions when we think the answer will be *yes*, e.g. in offers and requests.

   We use *some* and *any* with both uncountable nouns (e.g. *money*) and plural countable nouns (e.g. *oranges*).

▷   20.21 without a noun; 20.22 + *of*

20.15 Quantifiers: **every, each** and **any**

1 There is a prize-giving **every** year.
   Every pupil has to be there.

2 One pupil from **each** class gets a prize.
   Each prize-winner can choose a book.

3 You can choose **any** book you like.
   Anyone can enter the competition.

1 We use *every* to talk about what the speaker sees as a large indefinite number of people or things. *Every pupil* = all the pupils.

2 We use *each* to talk about the individual people or things in a group. The group has a definite (and often small) number. ▷ 20.23

3 We use *any* to talk about one person or thing (but it doesn't matter which one) from a large indefinite number. *any book* = it doesn't matter which book; any book you like.
   When *any* has this meaning, it is stressed.
   Compounds with *any-* can also have the same meaning (*anyone* = it doesn't matter who).
   any is also the negative of *some*. ▷ 20.14

20.16 Compounds with **every-, some-, any-** and **no-**

1 **Everyone/Everybody** likes Alan.
   Someone/Somebody has left their bag here.
   Has **anyone/anybody** seen Dick?
   No one/Nobody told me.

2 Have you got **everything**?
   There's **something** in my shoe.
   Did you buy **anything**?
   We've got **nothing** to do.

3 I've looked **everywhere** for the key.
   It must be **somewhere**.
   I haven't seen it **anywhere**.
   It's **nowhere** here.

4 Dick isn't here, but **everyone else** is.
   (= all the other people)
   There's **something else** that I've forgotten.
   (= another thing)

5 Is there **anything interesting** on television?
   There's **nowhere nice** to go for a walk here.

1 We use *-one/-body* to talk about people.
2 We use *-thing* to talk about things.
3 We use *-where* to talk about place.
4 We can use *else* after these compounds.
5 We can use an adjective after these compounds.

   We use *any-* in negative sentences and questions. ▷ 20.14 But ▷ 20.15

   Note In informal speech Americans sometimes use *everyplace, someplace, anyplace* and *noplace* instead of *everywhere* etc.

20.17 Quantifiers: **a lot of/lots of, many, much, a few, a little**

Countable nouns

a lot of/lots of *(a large number)*

1 I've got **a lot of** records.
Lots of people came.

many *(a large number)*

2 How **many** books have you got?
Have you got **many** books?/a lot of books?

3 I haven't got **many** books./a lot of books.

4 I've got **too many** stamps.
I've got **as many** as I need.

a few *(a small number)*

5 I've only got **a few** tins.

Uncountable nouns

a lot of/lots of *(a large amount)*
There's **a lot of** bread here.
We've got **lots of** time.

much *(a large amount)*
How **much** beer is there?
Is there **much** beer?/a lot of beer?
There isn't **much** beer./a lot of beer.
That's **too much** wine for me.
I've got **as much** as you.

a little *(a small amount)*
There's only **a little** butter.

1 We use *a lot of* or *lots of* in positive sentences with both countable and uncountable nouns.

2 We usually use *many* and *much* in questions (but we sometimes use *a lot of* if we think the answer will be *yes*).
We use *many* with countable nouns and *much* with uncountable nouns.

3 We usually use *many* and *much* in negative sentences (but we sometimes use *a lot of* in informal English).

4 We use *many* and *much* after *too, as, so* and *very*.

5 We use *a few* with countable nouns and *a little* with uncountable nouns.

20.18   Quantifiers: **more, most; fewer, fewest; less, least**

Countable nouns

more *(a larger number)*
Our team has won **more** games than your team.

most *(the largest number)*
We've won the **most** games.
(= more games than anyone else)

fewer/less *(a smaller number)*
You've won **fewer** games/**less** games than we have.
(= You haven't won as many games as we have.)

fewest/least *(the smallest number)*
You've won the **fewest** games/the **least** games.
(= fewer/less games than anyone else)

Uncountable nouns

more *(a larger amount)*
You've got **more** money than I have.

most *(the largest amount)*
You've got the **most** money.
(= more money than anyone else)

less *(a smaller amount)*
I've got **less** money than you have.
(= I haven't got as much money as you have.)

least *(the smallest amount)*
I've got the **least** money.
(= less money than anyone else)

We use *more* and *most* with both countable and uncountable nouns.
With countable nouns we use *fewer/fewest* (or *less/least* in informal English).
With uncountable nouns we use *less/least*.

20.19   **some more, another** and **other/others**

1   **some more**
Would you like **some more** sandwiches?
Have **some more** tea.

2   **another**
Would you like **another** sandwich?
Have you got these shoes in **another** colour?

3   **other/others**
They crossed to the **other** side of the road.
Kate's here, but where are the **others**?
I like this cheese better than the **other**.

1   *some more* = an extra quantity or amount
We use *some more* with both countable and uncountable nouns.

2   *another* = an extra one or a different one
We use *another* with countable nouns.

3   *other* = different
We use *other* with both countable and uncountable nouns.

20.20 **enough** and **plenty of**

Are there **enough** chairs for everyone?
I hope we've got **enough** petrol.
They took **plenty of** warm clothes.
Don't worry. We've got **plenty of** time.

We use *enough* and *plenty of* with both countable and uncountable nouns.

plenty of = more than enough

20.21 Quantifiers without a noun

With plural nouns
I need some potatoes. Can you lend me **some**?
We haven't got **any** in the house.
Have you got any old newspapers? ~
Well, not **a lot**, but I can give you **a few**. How **many** do you want?
I'm looking for some pins. There are **none** in the drawer.

With uncountable nouns
I need some sugar. Can you lend me **some**? We haven't got **any** in the house.
Can I borrow some ink? ~ I haven't got **a lot**, but I can give you **a little**. How **much** do you want?
I can't find any oil. There's **none** in the garage.

We can leave out a noun after a quantifier when the meaning is clear without it.
For *no* and *none* ▷ 20.23

20.22 Quantifiers + **of**

With plural nouns
We broke **some of** the eggs.
A few of my friends are coming round; you've met **two of** them before.
One of the windows was open.

With uncountable or singular nouns
Try **a little of** this cheese.
None of this wood is any use.
I saw **some of** the programme, but I missed **a lot of** it.

We use *of* when we talk about a quantity (e.g. *some*) which is part of a definite and limited quantity, e.g. *the eggs (in this box), my friends.*

▷   20.17 *a lot of*; 20.23

20.23 **all, most, both, either, neither, each, half** and **no/none**

1a **All** parties are exciting, I think.
b **All the** guests/**All of the** guests are here.
c Those magazines are **all** old. I've read them **all/all of** them.
d I've spent **all my** money/**all of my** money. He's drunk **all this** bottle/**all of this** bottle.
e He's drunk **this whole** bottle/**the whole of this** bottle.

1a *all* = every ▷ 20.15
   all + noun (without *the*) has a general meaning. *All parties* = every party in the world.
b *all the* + noun and *all of the* + noun have a more limited meaning. *All (of) the guests* = every guest at this party.
c We can use *all* in mid position or after an object pronoun.
d We can use *all* with uncountable and singular nouns as well as with plural nouns. We can use it with *my, your* etc. and with *this, that* etc.
e We can use *whole* with a singular noun with the same meaning as *all*.

2a **Most** people like parties.
b **Most of the** guests were students.
c Bob spends **most of his** time here.

2a *most* = more than half
   most + noun (without *the*) has a general meaning. *Most people* = most people in the world.
b *most of the* + noun has a more limited meaning. *Most of the guests* = most of the guests at this party.
c We can use *most* with uncountable nouns and singular nouns as well as with plural nouns. We can use it with *my, your* etc. and with *this, that* etc. ▷ 24.11 *most/mostly*

3a **Both** windows/**Both the** windows/**Both of the** windows are open.
b The windows are **both** open. I left them **both/both of** them open.
c **Both these** plates are broken.

3a We use *both* to talk about two things or two people. We can say *both* + noun, *both the* + noun or *both of the* + noun.
b We can use *both* in mid position or after an object pronoun.
c We can use *both* with *these* and *those*, and with *my, your* etc.

4a We can go **either** way, right or left.
b **Neither** box was big enough.
c I don't like **either of the** twins.
Neither of these boxes was/were big enough.

4a We use *either* and *neither* to talk about two things or two people. *either* = the one or the other.
b *neither* has a negative meaning. *Neither box was big enough* = both boxes were too small.
We can say *either/neither* + singular noun.
c We can also say *either of the/neither of the* + plural noun.
We can use *these* and *those* and *my, your* etc.
▷ 27.5 giving alternatives

5a **Each** child/**Each of the** children had a present.
b The children **each** had a present. We gave them **each/each of** them a present.
c These pens cost 60p **each**.

5a We use *each* to talk about the individual things or people in a group. ▷ 20.15
We can say *each* + singular noun or *each of the* + plural noun.
b We can use *each* in mid position or after an object pronoun.
c We can use *each* in end position.

6a **Half the** shops/**Half of the** shops were shut.
b I've read **half this** book/**half of this** book.
c **Half a** pound of butter, please.

6a We can say *half the* + noun or *half of the* + noun.
b We can use *half* with singular nouns and uncountable nouns as well as with plural nouns.
We can use it with *this, that* etc. and with *my, your* etc.
c We can say *half a/an* + noun.
▷ 24.8 *half* as an adverb

7a We had **no** milk and **no** eggs.
b There's **no** telephone in here.
c I wanted some eggs, but there were **none** at the shops.
d I dropped the eggs, but luckily **none of** them broke.
e **None of my** friends live in London.

7a *no* has a negative meaning. *We had no milk* = we hadn't any milk. *no* is more emphatic than *not any*.
b We can use *no* with singular nouns as well as with uncountable and plural nouns.
c We cannot use *no* without a noun. We use *none* instead.
d We cannot use *no + of*. We use *none* instead.
e We can use *my, your* etc. and *this, that* etc. after *none of*.

21 Question words

21.1 what, who, where, when, why, how and whose

1a **What** are you doing? ~ I'm looking for something.
b **Who** told you? ~ Peter.
c **Where** is the manager? ~ In London.
d **When** did this happen? ~ Yesterday afternoon.
e **Why** have you come? ~
Because I want to talk to you.
f **How** did you get here? ~ By car.
How long did it take? ~ About an hour.
g **Whose** (dog) is that? ~ It's mine.
2 **What else** would you like? (= What other things?)
Who else is coming? (= What other people?)

1a *what* asks about actions or things.
b *who* asks about people.
c *where* asks about place.
d *when* asks about time.
e *why* asks about reason or purpose.
f *how* asks about means, manner or degree. Also
▷ 29.2, 3 introductions, meeting someone
g *whose* asks about possession.
2 We can use *else* after these question words.

21.2 what and who asking about the subject and object

1 *Asking about the subject*
What's making that noise? ~
The washing-machine.
Who knows the answer? ~ No one does.
Who invited you? ~ Ben invited me.

2 *Asking about the object*
What's David making? ~ A table.
Who do you know here? ~ Well, I know Nicola.
Who did you invite? ~ Oh, a few friends.

1 When *what* or *who* asks about the subject, the verb is the same as in a statement, e.g. *is making, knows, invited.*
2 When *what* or *who* asks about the object, an auxiliary or modal verb comes before the subject. We use a form of *do* in the simple present or simple past tense.

21.3 **who, what** and **which**

1   **Who**'s your favourite film star? ~ Paul Newman.
2a **What**'s your favourite sport? ~ Golf.
 b **What** sport do you like best? ~ I like golf.
 c **What** instruments do you play? ~
    I play the guitar and the violin.
3a **Which** do you play best, the guitar or the violin?
 b **Which** box are your photos in? ~ This one here.
 c **Which** photos/**Which** ones did you take in
    Germany? ~ The ones on this page.
    Which of these girls/**Which** one is your friend? ~
    The one on the left.

Form

1   *who* is always without a noun.
2   *what* can be
a   without a noun
b   with a singular noun
c   with a plural noun
3   *which* can be
a   without a noun
b   with a singular noun
c   with a plural noun, with *one/ones* (▷ 20.13) or with
    of (▷ 20.22)

Use

1   *who* asks about people.
2   *what* asks about things.
3   *which* asks about things or people.

We use *who, what* or *which* when there is a
number of possible answers to choose from.

We use *who* or *what* when there is an indefinite
(and often very large) number of possible
answers, or when we do not know the possible
answers.

We use *which* when there is a limited (and often
very small) number of possible answers to choose
from.

21.4   Question phrases with **what** and **how**

What time did you leave? ~ Half past five.
What colour is the carpet? ~ Green.
What kind of/sort of shop is it? ~
It's a newsagent's.
I'm hungry. **What about** you? ~ Yes, me too.
How much is this table? ~ Sixty pounds.
How many children have they got? ~ Two, I think.
How old is Mr Hall? ~ Oh, about forty.
How often do you go out? ~ About once a week.

We use these question phrases to ask about the details of a person, a thing or an action.

▷   20.17 *how much/how many*

21.5   Prepositions in questions

1   **Which** office is Pat ⬚working **in**⬚ now?
Pat is ⬚working **in**⬚ the small office now.

Who did you ⬚speak **to**⬚ ?
We ⬚spoke **to**⬚ the manager.

2   **In which** office is Pat working now?
3   **To whom** did you speak?
4   **What** did she want you **for**? ~
Oh, nothing important.
5   **What**'s she **like**? ~ She's very nice.

1   In a question we usually put a preposition in the same place as in a statement.
2   In more formal or written English we can put a preposition at the beginning of a question.
3   We use *whom* instead of *who* after a preposition. *whom* is formal and not often used in spoken English.
4   *What . . . for?* = Why?
5   *What . . . like?* asks a question that we can answer with an adjective.

22 Relative clauses

22.1 Relative pronouns and relative clauses

1 The boy **who comes from Bristol** won the game.
The sport **that I like watching** is tennis.

2 Peter Oates, **who comes from Bristol**, won the game.
The first game, **which went on for a long time**, wasn't very exciting.

A relative clause (e.g. *who comes from Bristol*) begins with a relative pronoun (e.g. *who, that*). But ▷ 22.4, 10, 11

A relative clause comes after a noun phrase (e.g. *the boy, the sport*).

1 Most relative clauses are *defining clauses*, e.g. *who comes from Bristol* (without commas). ▷ 22.12. The relative clauses in 22.2–11 are defining clauses.

2 Some relative clauses are *non-defining clauses*, e.g. *who comes from Bristol* (with commas). ▷ 22.12–14

22.2 The relative pronouns **who** and **which**

1 The girl **who works at the café** is Martin's sister.
Is that the café **which stays open till ten**?

2 Martin is the man **who we saw yesterday**.
Did you see the motor-bike **which he bought for £20**?

who and *which* are relative pronouns. We use *who* with people and *which* with things.

who and *which* can be

1 the subject of a relative clause (*The girl* works at the café. *The café* stays open till ten.)

2 the object of the relative clause (We saw *the man* yesterday. He bought *the motor-bike* for £20.)

22.3 The relative pronoun **that**

1 Is this the train **that stops at Shenfield**?
Here's the newspaper **that I found on the seat**.

2 Do you know the man **that sat next to us yesterday**?
The woman **that you helped** is our neighbour.

We can use the relative pronoun *that* instead of *who* or *which*.

1 We mostly use *that* to talk about things.

2 We sometimes use *that* to talk about people, but we use *who* much more often. ▷ 22.2

22.4   Relative clauses without a pronoun: leaving out **who, which** or **that**

1   Martin is the man **who we saw yesterday**.
    Martin is the man **we saw yesterday**.
    Did you see the motor-bike **which he bought for £20**?
    Did you see the motor-bike **he bought for £20**?

2   His sister works in the café **that we went to**.
    His sister works in the café **we went to**.

We can leave out *who, which* or *that*

1   when it is the object of a relative clause (You saw *the man* yesterday. He bought *the motor-bike* for £20.)

2   when there is a preposition (We went *to the café*.) ▷ 22.5

We cannot leave out *who, which* or *that* when it is the subject of a relative clause.

22.5   Prepositions in relative clauses

1   A girl **who** [I used to go out **with**] lives near here.
    [I used to go out **with**] a girl.

2   Here's the map **that** [you were looking **for**]
    [You were looking **for**] the map.

3   The article [you were talking **about**] earlier is in this magazine.
    [You were talking **about**] the article.

In a relative clause we put a preposition in the same place as in a main clause. We do not usually put it before the relative pronoun. But ▷ 22.7

We can use a preposition in a relative clause

1   with *who* or *which*

2   with *that*

3   without a pronoun

▷   21.5 prepositions in questions

22.6   The relative pronoun **whom**

1   The woman **who they interviewed yesterday** has been given the job.
    The woman **whom they interviewed yesterday** has been given the job.

2   The people **who we stayed with** are old friends.
    The people **whom we stayed with** are old friends.

We use *who* and *whom* to talk about people.

We can use *whom* instead of *who*

1   when it is the object of the relative clause (They interviewed *the woman* yesterday.)

2   when there is a preposition (We stayed *with some old friends*.) ▷ 22.7

whom is more formal than *who* and is not often used in spoken English.

22.7 A preposition at the beginning of a relative clause

1 The person **who** I spoke **to** earlier isn't there now.
It's a problem **which** we can do very little **about**.

2 The person **to whom** I spoke earlier isn't there now.
It's a problem **about which** we can do very little.

1 In a relative clause we usually put a preposition in the same place as in a main clause. This is the normal order in informal spoken English. ▷ 22.5

2 In more formal or written English we can put a preposition at the beginning of a relative clause.
If we put a preposition at the beginning, we use *whom* or *which*. We cannot use the relative pronouns *who* or *that* after a preposition.

22.8 The relative pronoun **whose**

1 Workers **whose** wages are low should be paid more.
2 We are a nation **whose** wealth comes mainly from industry.
3 'Lively Lady' was the horse **whose** jockey fell.
4 That's the farm **whose** owner went to Australia.

We use *whose* to talk about possession.
whose can refer to

1 people
2 countries
3 animals
4 things

Note We also use *of which* to talk about things, e.g. *That's the farm the owner of which went to Australia.* In informal speech we often express the meaning in a different way, e.g. *The owner of that farm went to Australia.*

22.9 The relative pronoun **what**

We've found out **what** we need to know.
You never let me do **what** I want to do.

what we need to know = the thing that we need to know.

▷ 27.3 *what* in a clause used as subject or object;
28.5 *what* used for emphasis

22.10 Relative clauses without a pronoun: the infinitive

1   Gary was **the first** person **to arrive** and **the last to leave**.
    (= . . . the first person who arrived and the last one who left.)
2   Jill was **the only** one **to remember** my birthday.
    (= . . . the only one who remembered . . .)
3   Your party was **the most exciting** thing **to happen** here for months.
    (= . . . the most exciting thing that's happened here . . .)

We can use the infinitive instead of a relative pronoun and a verb
1   after *the first, the second* etc. and *the next*
2   after *the only*
3   after superlatives

22.11 Relative clauses without a pronoun: the -ing form and the -ed form

1   People **wanting** to make an enquiry should go to the office.
    (= People who want to make an enquiry . . .)
2   The men **building** the houses were well paid.
    (= The men who were building the houses . . .)
3   New homes **offered** for sale today are sold very quickly.
    (= New homes which are offered for sale . . .)
4   A house **bought** ten years ago is worth much more today.
    (= A house which was bought ten years ago . . .)

1,2   We can use an -ing form instead of a relative pronoun and an active verb.
3,4   We can use an -ed form instead of a relative pronoun and a passive verb.

The -ing form or the -ed form can replace a verb
1,3   in a present tense or
2,4   in a past tense

22.12 Defining and non-defining relative clauses

1   *Defining relative clauses*
    The man **who has worked here for 45 years** is retiring next month.
    The company **he works for** is Wilson and Sons.

1   Most relative clauses are defining clauses. The clause *who has worked here for 45 years* defines the man (tells us *which* man).
    The defining clause is necessary to understand the meaning of the main clause. There is no pause or comma before a defining relative clause.

2 *Non-defining relative clauses*
Mr Rose, **who has worked here for 45 years**, is retiring next month.
Wilson and Sons, **for whom he has worked since he was 20**, have been in existence since 1823.
The manager (**whose wife was also there**) handed a beautiful old clock to Mr Rose.
The clock—**which cost over £100**—was paid for by the people at the factory.

3 *Compare the use of two main clauses*
Mr Rose has worked here for 45 years, and he's retiring next month.

2 Some relative clauses are non-defining clauses. The clause *who has worked here for 45 years* adds extra information about Mr Rose. It does not define Mr Rose—we already know who he is.

We can leave out the non-defining clause and still have a sentence which means something.

There is a comma before and after a non-defining relative clause. The clause is sometimes in brackets or between dashes.

We form non-defining relative clauses with *who, whom, whose* or *which*. We do not use *that* in non-defining clauses.

Non-defining relative clauses are rather formal.

3 In informal spoken English we normally use two main clauses instead of a main clause and a non-defining relative clause.

22.13 **why, when** and **where**

1 I've forgotten the reason **why** we went to Bournemouth.
. . . the reason we went to Bournemouth.
I'll never forget the day **when** we arrived there.
. . . the day we arrived there.
Do you remember the hotel **where** we stayed?
. . . the hotel we stayed at?

2 We went in May, **when** it's normally quiet.
We stopped at Ashford, **where** there's that nice pub by the canal.

1 We can use *why, when* and *where* in a defining relative clause. We can leave out *why* or *when*.
We can also leave out *where*, but then we must use a preposition, e.g. *the hotel we stayed at.*

2 We can form non-defining relative clauses with *when* and *where*.
We cannot leave out *when* and *where* from a non-defining clause.

22.14 **which** referring to a whole clause

I was late again this morning, **which** made my boss angry.
The telephone wasn't working, **which** was an awful nuisance.

We can use *which* to talk about a whole clause, e.g. *I was late again this morning.*

These relative clauses with *which* are non-defining clauses.

23 Adjectives

23.1 Introduction to adjectives

1 We've got an **old** house.
I like **old** houses.
2 This is a **nice** coat.
This coat is **nice**.
3 The boys are **afraid** of the dark.
The driver was still **alive**.

Form

1 An adjective has the same form in the singular and in the plural, e.g. *an old house, old houses.*
2 An adjective comes before a noun (*a nice coat*) or after *be* (*. . . is nice*). And ▷ 24.12
3 A few adjectives come after *be* but do not normally come before a noun. Examples: *afraid, alive, alone, asleep, awake, ill, well.*

Use

An adjective describes (tells us something about) a noun.

23.2 The regular comparison of adjectives

1 This radio's **cheap**. It's only £10.
This one's **cheaper** than that. It's only £7.50.
This must be **the cheapest** one. It's only £4.75.
2 This is an **expensive** coat. It's £80.
I can't afford a **more expensive** coat.
This one is the **most expensive** of all. It's £120.
3a You're taller **than Bob.**/**than Bob is**.
b You're taller **than him.**/**than he is**.
4a Which is the longest bridge **in the world**?
b It's the most exciting book **I've ever read**.

1 Short adjectives of one syllable (e.g. *cheap, tall, nice*) take *-er* in the comparative (*cheaper*) and *-est* in the superlative (*cheapest*). But ▷ 23.3
For spelling (e.g. *nicer, bigger, happier*) ▷ 38.3, 5, 6
2 Longer adjectives of three or more syllables (e.g. *expensive, interesting, dangerous*) take *more* in the comparative (*more expensive*) and *most* in the superlative (*most expensive*).
3a After the comparative form we can use *than*. After *than* we can put a noun phrase (*than Bob*) or a noun phrase + verb (*than Bob is*).
b A personal pronoun without a verb after *than* has the object form (*than him*).
4 After a superlative we often use
a a phrase with a preposition
b a relative clause without a pronoun ▷ 22.4

Note on adjectives of two syllables

These adjectives usually take **-er/-est** (but they can take **more/most**):

silly	sillier	the silliest
simple	simpler	the simplest
clever	cleverer	the cleverest
quiet	quieter	the quietest

Also: *funny, dirty* etc.; *gentle, feeble* etc.
Adjectives in *-ed* usually take *more/most*, even adjectives of one syllable. Some examples: *tired, bored, amused, annoyed, surprised*.

Most other two-syllable adjectives take **more/most**:

careful	more careful	the most careful
boring	more boring	the most boring
modern	more modern	the most modern
correct	more correct	the most correct
famous	more famous	the most famous

Also: *useful, hopeful* etc.; *tiring, willing* etc.
With these adjectives either *-er/-est* or *more/most* is used: *polite, stupid, narrow, pleasant, common, handsome.*

23.3   The irregular comparison of adjectives

1   Nottingham has some **good** shops.
Sheffield is **better** for shopping.
The shops in Manchester are **best**.

2   Thursday is market day. It's a **bad** day for parking.
The problem is **worse** in summer.
Saturday is the **worst** time of the week.

Form

| 1 | **good** | **better** | **the best** |
| 2 | **bad** | **worse** | **the worst** |

▷   24.14 irregular comparison of adverbs

23.4   Comparison: **as . . . as** and **so . . . as**

1   The train is just **as** expensive **as** the plane. They both cost £85.
Unfortunately the news was **as** bad **as** we had expected.

2   Today isn't **as** cold **as** yesterday.
Today isn't **so** cold **as** yesterday.

3   Everything is just the same **as** before, really.

1   In positive sentences we use *as . . . as* to compare two things that are the same in some way.

2   In negative sentences we use either *as . . . as* or *so . . . as*.

3   We also use *as* after *the same*. Compare *different from* (▷ 25.12).

23.5 Comparison: **less, least**

These shoes are expensive. They're £30.
The black ones are **less** expensive. They're £20.
These here are the **least** expensive. They're £10.

less and *least* are the opposites of *more* and *most*.
▷ 23.2

23.6 Comparatives with **and**

The queue of people was getting **longer and longer**.
I began to feel **more and more nervous**.

We can repeat a comparative after *and* to talk about a change happening over a period of time.

23.7 Comparatives with **the**

The higher our wages, **the better** our standard of living.
The smaller a garden is, **the easier** it is to look after.

We use *the* + comparative to talk about a change in one thing which causes a change in something else.

23.8 **latest, last; nearest, next; further, farther**

1   The M7 is our **latest** motorway. It was opened only last week.
The M7 will be the **last** motorway. There's no money to build any more.

2   There are no garages here. The **nearest** one is 25 miles away.
You'd better get some petrol at this garage. The **next** one is 25 miles away.

3   How much **further/farther** is it to Glasgow?
Let's hope there are no **further** problems.

1   *latest* = newest
last = final (but *last week* = the week before this)

2   *nearest* = closest, least far
next = the one after this

3   *further/farther* = longer in distance
further = more

23.9 **the** + adjective

1 **The rich** are healthier than **the poor**.
2 You've got to take **the good** with **the bad**.

1 We use *the* + adjective to talk about a whole group of people, e.g. *the young, the old, the sick, the unemployed. The rich* = rich people.
2 We also use *the* + adjective to talk about abstract ideas, e.g. *the new, the unknown, the absurd.*

23.10 Nationality words

1a I've bought some **Italian** shoes.
b Can you speak **Italian**?
c The owner is an **Italian**.
d **Italians/The Italians** are very artistic.
2a It's a **Japanese** radio.
b I'm trying to learn **Japanese**.
c A lot of **Japanese** come here in summer.
d The **Japanese** sell lots of things to Europe.
3a Was it an **English** film?
b My **English** is getting better.
c There was an **Englishman** opposite me.
d **Englishmen/The English** love dogs.

We can use a nationality word
a as an adjective
b as the name of a language
c to talk about a person or a group of people
d to talk about a nation as a whole
1c Some of the words for people are nouns with a singular and a plural form, e.g. *Italian(s), American(s), Brazilian(s), Swede(s).*
2c Some of the words for people are adjectives which we also use as nouns, e.g. *Japanese, Chinese, Portuguese, Swiss.* They can have a singular or a plural meaning.
3d We can refer to some nations by using either a noun or an adjective, e.g. *Englishmen/the English, Irishmen/the Irish, Frenchmen/the French, Spaniards/the Spanish.*

We can also use an adjective to refer to people, or nations, e.g. *They're Spanish. She's a French girl. English people love dogs.*

▷ 19.4 *a/an*

24 Adverbs

24.1 Types of adverbs

1 *Adverbs of manner* ▷24.5
The children walked home **quickly**.
They ate their supper **hungrily**.

2 *Adverbs of place and time* ▷ 24.6
Mr Barnes is going to have lunch **here**.
You can speak to him **then**.

3 *Adverbs of frequency* ▷ 24.7
The Smiths **often** visit us.
They **usually** come on Sundays.

4 *Adverbs of degree* ▷ 24.8
I'm **very** tired.
I had to get up **really** early.
I **almost** fell asleep this afternoon.

5 *Sentence adverbs* ▷ 24.9
Maybe I'll come and see you.
It'll **probably** be OK.
I'm not very busy just now, **luckily**.

6 *Prepositional adverbs* ▷ 26.1
The Browns weren't **in**.
(=They weren't in the house.)
The car stopped and a woman got **out**.
(= A woman got out of the car.)

We use an adverb
1 to say *how* something happens
2 to say *where* or *when* something happens
3 to say *how often* something happens
4 to make the meaning of an adjective, adverb or verb *stronger* or *weaker*
5 to refer to a whole sentence and show what the speaker thinks about the sentence
6 Some adverbs are like prepositions without a noun phrase after them.

24.2   Adverb forms

1a   It'll be eight o'clock **soon**.
 b   Alan is **always** late.
 c   He wasn't **so** late last week.
 d   **Perhaps** he isn't coming.
2a   We'll have to walk **fast**.
 b   We had to leave **early** this morning.
3a   We'll have to walk **quickly**.
 b   It's been very warm **recently**.
 c   I **usually** see her at lunch time.
 d   We're **nearly** at the house now.
 e   It's a bit further, **actually**.
4a   The woman was friendly. She spoke **in a friendly way**.
 b   Rain is likely. It's **probably** going to rain.

1   Some adverbs have no special form. These adverbs are
a   most adverbs of time and place ▷ 24.6
b   some adverbs of frequency ▷ 24.7
c   some adverbs of degree ▷ 24.8
d   some sentence adverbs ▷ 24.9
2   Some adverbs have the same form as adjectives. These adverbs are
a   some adverbs of manner
b   some adverbs of time
▷   24.10
3   We form some adverbs from an adjective + -*ly*. These adverbs are
a   most adverbs of manner ▷ 24.5
b   some adverbs of time ▷ 24.6
c   some adverbs of frequency ▷ 24.7
d   some adverbs of degree ▷ 24.8
e   most sentence adverbs ▷ 24.9
▷   38.3, 6 spelling
4   We cannot form an adverb from an adjective which ends in -*ly*. Instead we can use
a   the phrase *in a . . . way*/*manner* or
b   an adverb of similar meaning.
      But ▷ 24.10 *early*

24.3   Adverb phrases

She thanked us **with a smile**.
The game is **next Saturday**.
I see Alex **from time to time**.
We enjoyed the party **very much indeed**.
In actual fact, the story was untrue.

An adverb is sometimes a whole phrase, not just one word.

24.4   The position of adverbs

There are three places in the sentence where adverbs can come.

1   Front position

Adverb	Subject + verb	
a	**Yesterday**	the team played	well.
b	**Usually**	I go	to the café.
c	**Perhaps**	I'll see	you later.

1   Front position is at the beginning of the sentence.

These kinds of adverbs go in front position:
a   sometimes adverbs or adverb phrases of time and place ▷ 24.6
b   sometimes adverbs of frequency ▷ 24.7
c   sometimes sentence adverbs ▷ 24.9

▷   28.3 front position for emphasis

2   Mid position

Subject	(Auxiliary or modal verb)	Adverb	(Verb)	
a	He		**slowly**	opened	the door.
	I		**usually**	go	to the café.
b	I	don't	**really**	like	fish.
	We	've	**just**	finished	the painting.
c	The story	is	**certainly**		very exciting.

2   Mid position is
a   before a verb in the simple present or simple past tense
b   after the first auxiliary or modal verb in the verb phrase
c   after be

These kinds of adverbs go in mid position:
a   sometimes adverbs of manner ▷ 24.5 adverbs of frequency ▷ 24.7
b   some adverbs of degree ▷ 24.8 sometimes a few adverbs of time ▷ 24.6
c   sometimes sentence adverbs ▷ 24.9

3 End position

	Subject + verb	(Direct object)	
a	They talked		**quietly**.
b	He opened	the door	**slowly**.
c	City played		**well at York yesterday**.
d	Ben danced		**a lot with that tall girl**.
e	I go		**to the café usually**.
f	I'll see	you	**later, perhaps**.

3 End position is

a after the verb (if there is no direct object)

b after the verb + direct object

Sometimes there is more than one adverb or phrase in end position.

c The normal order is manner (e.g. *well*) + place (e.g. *at York*) + time (e.g. *yesterday*).

d We often put a short phrase (e.g. *a lot*) before a longer phrase (e.g. *with that tall girl*).

e In end position an adverb of frequency usually comes after an adverb or adverb phrase of place.

f A sentence adverb usually comes at the end of the sentence, sometimes after a comma.

In end position we put

a,b,c adverbs of manner ▷ 24.5

c sometimes adverbs or adverb phrases of time and place ▷ 24.6

d some adverbs of degree ▷ 24.8

e sometimes adverbs of frequency ▷ 24.7

f sometimes sentence adverbs ▷ 24.9

24.5 Adverbs of manner

1	*Adjective*	The journey was very **slow**.
	Adverb	We travelled **slowly**.
2	*Adjective*	Mr Harris is a **careful** driver.
	Adverb	He drives his car very **carefully**.
3	*Adjective*	The climb up the hill was **easy**.
	Adverb	We **easily** climbed the hill.
4	*Adjective*	The singing was **loud**.
	Adverb	They sang **loudly/loud**.

1 An adjective (e.g. *slow*) describes a noun (e.g. *journey*). An adverb of manner (e.g. *slowly*) describes a verb (e.g. *travelled*).

An adverb of manner ends in *-ly*. ▷ 38.3, 6 spelling. But the adverb of *good* is *well*. And ▷ 24.11 *high*, *near* etc.

2 An adverb of manner usually comes at the end of a sentence. Do not put it between the verb and the direct object.

3 An adverb of manner sometimes has mid position.

4 In informal English and in American English an adjective is sometimes used instead of an adverb. In British English this happens especially with *loud, cheap, slow* and *quick*.

24.6 Place and time

1 **At the disco** they played my favourite records.
Yesterday they played my favourite records.
They played my favourite records **at the disco**.
They played my favourite records **yesterday**.

2 They played my favourite records **at the disco yesterday**.
We went **there on Saturday evening**.

3 Bob will **soon** be here.
He's **just** arrived.

1 An adverb or adverb phrase of place or of time can usually come at the beginning or end of a sentence. Some more examples: *here*, *at home*, *in the street*, *over there*; *afterwards*, *again*, *tomorrow*, *last week*.

2 Place normally comes before time in end position.

3 A few adverbs of time can have mid position, e.g. *soon*, *just*, *already*, *now*, *then*.

▷ 24.16 *yet*, *still* and *already*

24.7 Adverbs of frequency

1 She **always** stays in bed on Sunday morning.
Have you **ever** been to Greece?
I **sometimes** listen to the news.

2 **Sometimes** I listen to the news.
I listen to the news **sometimes**.
Do you come here **often**?

3 **Every August** they went on holiday.
You have to pay the rent **every week**.
I go to the dentist **twice a year**.

Adverbs of frequency say how often something happens. Some examples: *always*, *often*, *usually*, *normally*, *sometimes*, *occasionally*, *ever*, *never*.

1 Adverbs of frequency usually have mid position.

2 *sometimes*, *usually*, *normally* and *occasionally* can also have front or end position. *often* can have end position.

3 Adverb phrases of frequency with *every* and with *a/an* usually have front or end position.
For *daily*, *hourly* etc. ▷ 24.10

▷ 19.6 *a/an* in phrases of price, speed etc.;
36.4 *once*, *twice* etc.

24.8 Adverbs of degree

With adjectives and adverbs

1 The music was **very** loud.
Why did it take **so** long?
The shelf is **too** high.

2 I'm not tall **enough**.

3 £25 is **very**/**extremely** expensive for a meal.
£15 is **rather**/**pretty**/**fairly**/**quite** expensive.
£10 is **a bit**/**a little** expensive.

4 The food was **quite**/**absolutely** excellent.
This book is **completely**/**totally** useless.

5 The stadium was **half** empty.
I'm **ninety-nine per cent** certain.

With comparatives

6 You need something **a bit**/**a little** bigger than that.
I did it **much**/**a lot** more easily the second time.
Is your mother **any** better today?

With verbs

7 I **just** love this record.
We **almost** had an accident.
I **completely** forgot about it.

8 I didn't like her first book very **much**, but I like this one **a lot**.

An adverb or adverb phrase of degree makes the meaning of an adjective, adverb or verb stronger or weaker.

1 An adverb of degree comes before the adjective or adverb it describes.

2 But *enough* comes after the adjective or adverb it describes.

3 *very* and *extremely* make the meaning of an adjective or adverb stronger; *rather, pretty, fairly* and *quite* make the meaning a little stronger; *a bit* and *a little* make the meaning weaker. *pretty* and *a bit* are rather informal.

4 We also use *quite* (and e.g. *absolutely, completely, totally*) to give emphasis to the meaning when the adjective or adverb already has a very strong meaning, e.g. *excellent* (= very good), *useless, awful, marvellous, perfect, right, wrong, correct, sure, impossible*.

5 We sometimes use a fraction or a percentage as an adverb of degree.

6 These adverbs can come before a comparative: *much, a lot, rather, a bit, a little, any, no.*

7 An adverb of degree that describes a verb has mid position, e.g. *just, almost, completely, quite, rather.*

8 But *much, a lot, a bit* and *a little* have end position when they describe a verb.

24.9 Sentence adverbs

Fortunately the weather was good.
Of course you can come.
We **certainly** need some help.
David will **probably** be there.
He won't be there, **actually**.
He isn't very well, **unfortunately**.

Sentence adverbs show what the speaker thinks about the sentence. *fortunately* means that the speaker is pleased about the weather.

Sentence adverbs can have front position, mid position or end position.

Some more examples: *in fact, really, surely, possibly, maybe, perhaps, naturally, (un)luckily.*

24.10   Adverbs with the same form as adjectives

1   *Adjective*   Mrs Wells is a **hard** worker.
     Adverb   She works very **hard**.

     Adjective   We were **early**.
     Adverb   We arrived **early**.

2   *Adjective*   The **daily** newspaper arrives at seven o'clock.

     Adverb   The newspaper arrives **daily** at seven o'clock.

1   *hard* and *early* are both adjectives and adverbs. Other adverbs with the same form as adjectives are *fast, high, low, deep, near, late* and *long*. But ▷ 24.11

2   *daily, hourly, weekly, monthly* and *yearly* are both adjectives and adverbs. We form them from the nouns *day, hour* etc.

24.11   **high, highly; near, nearly; hard, hardly; late, lately; most, mostly**

1   The balloon didn't go very **high**.
     I'm reading a **highly** amusing book.

2   The fish came quite **near**.
     I **nearly** caught one.

3   They worked very **hard**.
     They **hardly** had any time for lunch.

4   We arrived **late** because of bad weather.
     There have been a lot of storms **lately**.

5   What I hate **most** about air travel is waiting at airports.
     On long journeys I **mostly** travel by plane.

high, near, hard and *late* are adverbs with the same form as adjectives. ▷ 24.10

most is an adverb with the same form as a quantifier. ▷ 20.18

highly, nearly, hardly, lately and *mostly* are also adverbs, but they have different meanings from *high, near* etc.

1   *highly* = very
2   *nearly* = almost
3   *hardly any time* = almost no time
4   *lately* = recently, in the last few days/weeks
5   *mostly* = mainly, usually

24.12   Adjectives instead of adverbs after **feel, look** etc.

I feel **hungry**.
The garden looked very **nice**.
This pudding tastes **delicious**.

We use an adjective (not an adverb) when we can use *be* instead of the verb. *I feel hungry* means that I *am* hungry.

We use an adjective after *feel, look, taste, smell, sound, seem, appear, become, get* (= become) and *stay*.

24.13 The regular comparison of adverbs

1 Could you say that **more slowly**, please?
Tom can shoot the **most accurately**.

2 You'll just have to get up **earlier**.
Sarah ran the **fastest**.

3 Shout a bit **louder/more loudly**.
You can buy them **cheapest/most cheaply** at Scott's.

1 Adverbs in -ly form their comparative and superlative with *more* and *most*. (But note *earlier* in 2.)

2 Adverbs with the same form as adjectives form their comparative and superlative with -er and -est.

3 Some adjectives can be used instead of adverbs in informal English, e.g. *loud, cheap, slow, quick*.
▷ 24.5

24.14 The irregular comparison of adverbs

1 Adrian can draw very **well**.
He can draw **better** than I can.
He can draw animals **best**.

2 The team played **badly**.
They played **worse** than last week.
Jones played the **worst**.

3 Martin can't swim very **far**.
You can swim **further/farther** than Martin.
Sarah can swim the **furthest**/the **farthest**.

Form

1	**well**	**better**	**best**
2	**badly**	**worse**	**worst**
3	**far**	**further/farther**	**furthest/farthest**

▷ 23.3 irregular comparison of adjectives; 23.8 *further/farther*

24.15 Comparison: **as . . . as, less** etc.

I can't do crosswords **as quickly as** you.
The old man's son visits him **less often** nowadays.
They went **faster and faster** down the hill.
The more you practise, **the better** you'll play.

We use *as . . . as, less* etc. with adverbs as well as with adjectives. ▷ 23.4–7

24.16 **yet, still, already** and **no longer**

1 Has the letter come **yet**? ~ No, not **yet**.
We haven't seen our new neighbours **yet**.

2a Are you **still** waiting?
She's fifteen, but she **still** takes a teddy bear to
bed with her.

b The letter **still** hasn't come.

3a I've **already** done that exercise.
Have you **already** had lunch?

b I've done that exercise **already**. It was easy.
Have you had lunch **already**? It's only quarter past
twelve.

4a Mr Baker **no longer** lives here.

b He doesn't live here **any longer/any more**.

1 We use *yet* to talk about something we are
expecting.
We use *yet* in questions and in negative
statements.
yet comes at the end of a sentence.

2 We use *still* to talk about something going on
longer than we expected.
still comes

a in mid position in questions and positive
statements

b after the subject in negative statements

3 We use *already* to talk about something
happening sooner than we expected.
We use *already* mainly in positive statements and
in questions.
already comes

a in mid position

b at the end of the sentence if we want to give it
more emphasis

4 We use *no longer* and *any longer/any more* to talk
about something that has come to an end.

a *no longer* has a negative meaning. It comes in mid
position.

b We use *any longer/any more* in negative
statements. It comes at the end of a sentence.

24.17 **only** and **even**

1 The couple **only** stayed one night at the hotel.
  We could **only** get a cheese sandwich.

2 He's very active for an 80-year-old. He **even** plays golf.
  I can't **even** remember my own telephone number.

3 Some houses haven't got electricity **even** today.

4 **Only** tourists buy these things.
  Even the stupidest person could understand it.

5 The **only** food we could get was a cheese sandwich.

6 The couple stayed **only** one night at the hotel.

7 This car park is for customers **only**.

1 In informal English, *only* has mid position. It need not come next to the word that it refers to, e.g. *one*.

2 *even* also has mid position.

3 *even* can come before the word it refers to.

4 When *only* and *even* refer to the subject, they come before it.

5 We can also use *only* as an adjective.

6 In rather formal or careful English, *only* can come before the word or phrase that it refers to, e.g. *one*.

7 In official written English, e.g. on notices, *only* comes after the word or phrase that it refers to, e.g. *customers*.

24.18 **long** and **far**

1 Have you been here **long**?
  How **far** is it to Cambridge?
  I won't stay **long**.
  We didn't go **far**.

2 I've been waiting **a long time**.
  It's **a long way** to the park.

3 The meeting went on so **long** I missed my bus.
  It's too **far** to walk.

1 We normally use the adverbs *long* and *far* only in questions and negative statements.

2 We normally use *a long time* and *a long way* in positive statements.

3 But we use *long* and *far* after *too, so* and *as*, even in positive statements.

25 Prepositions

25.1 Prepositions of place and movement

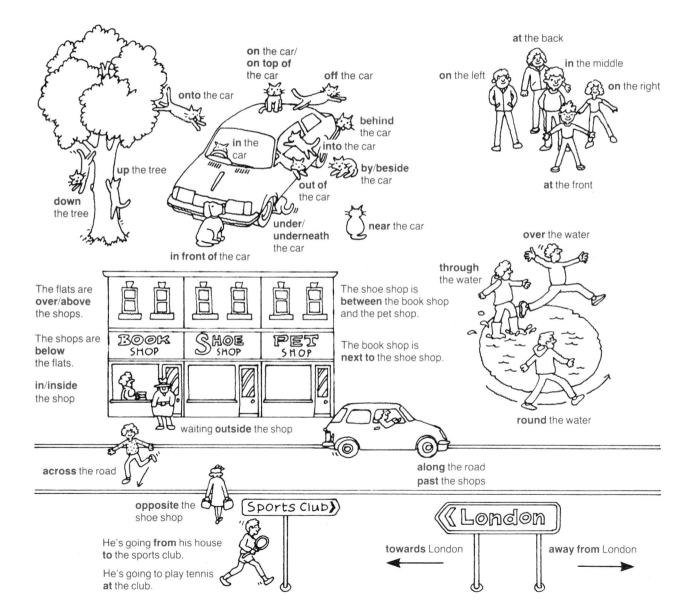

on the car/
on top of
the car

off the car

at the back

in the middle

on the left

on the right

onto the car

behind
the car

into the car

in the
car

up the tree

by/beside
the car

out of
the car

down
the tree

near the car

at the front

under/
underneath
the car

over the water

in front of the car

through
the water

The flats are
over/above
the shops.

The shoe shop is
between the book shop
and the pet shop.

The shops are
below
the flats.

BOOK SHOP

SHOE SHOP

PET SHOP

The book shop is
next to the shoe shop.

in/inside
the shop

round the water

waiting **outside** the shop

across the road

along the road
past the shops

opposite the
shoe shop

Sports Club

He's going **from** his house
to the sports club.

He's going to play tennis
at the club.

London

towards London

away from London

25.2   Prepositions of place: **at** and **in**

1   Simon was **at** the bus stop.
2   We live **at** 23 Bolton Road.
3   We were **at** the theatre.
    (= . . . watching a play.)
    The boys are **at** the swimming-pool.
    (= . . . swimming or watching the swimmers.)
4   We stopped **at** a village near Coventry.
5   The Jamesons live **at** Oxford.

1   Susan was **in** the garden.
2   We live **in** Bolton Road.
3   It was dark **in** the theatre.
    (= . . . inside the theatre.)
    It was cold **in** the swimming-pool.
    (= . . . in the water.)
4   There were two shops **in** the village.
5   The Jamesons live **in** Oxford.
6   They're on holiday **in** Spain.

We use *at* with

1   a position
2   a house or an address
3   a building (e.g. *theatre*), when we are thinking of the activity that takes place there
4   a village or town on a journey
5   a village or town (but *in* is more usual)

We use *in* (= inside) with

1   something big enough to be all around a person
2   a road or street
3   a building or other large space
4   a village
5   a town or city
6   a country

25.3   Prepositions of time: **at, on** and **in**

at
at four o'clock
at breakfast
at night
at Christmas
at the weekend
at that time

on
on Friday(s)
on Tuesday morning
on May 21st
on the next day

in
in the morning
in June
in summer
in 1985

No preposition
Is there a meeting this week?
I'll see you next Tuesday.
We went there last year.

In informal American English the preposition is also left out in e.g. *He'll be back Saturday.*

▷   19.9 phrases of time without *the*

25.4 Prepositions of time: **before, during** and **after**

The post office is very busy **before** Christmas.
I'm always out at work **during** the day.
We had to take a taxi home **after** the party.

We can also use *before* and *after* as conjunctions.
▷ 15.2; 27.2

during is a preposition; *while* is a conjunction with the same meaning. ▷ 15.2; 27.2

25.5 Prepositions of time: **till/until** and **by**

1   My mother's staying with us **till** Friday/**until** Friday.
2   Can you give me the money **by** the weekend?

1   *till Friday/until Friday* = from now to Friday.
till is more informal than *until*.

2   *by the weekend* = not later than the weekend.

▷   27.2 *till/until* as a conjunction

25.6 Prepositions of time: **from . . . to/till/until**

The sale was **from** December 28th **to** January 3rd.
The shop is open **from** nine **till** five thirty.
It will be closed **from** tomorrow **until** next Tuesday.

We use *from . . . to/till/until* to talk about the beginning and end of a period of time.
Americans use *from . . . through*, e.g. *It will be closed from tomorrow through next Tuesday.*

25.7 Prepositions of time: **for, since** and **in**; the adverb **ago**

1   I've only had this watch (**for**) six months.
Dick's going to France **for** a year.
2   I've only had this watch **since** March.
I haven't seen Julia **since** Christmas.
3   I bought this watch six months **ago**.
Shakespeare was born over four hundred years **ago**.
4a   Dick will be leaving for France **in** two days.
b   He ran the mile **in** 3 minutes 55 seconds.

1   We use *for* with a period of time, e.g. *six months*.
We can sometimes leave out *for*.

2   We use *since* with a point of time, e.g. *March*.
since March = from March to now.

3   We use *ago* for past time measured from the present. *six months ago* = six months before now.

4   We use *in* to talk about
a   a point of future time measured from the present.
in two days = two days from now.
b   a period of time needed to do something.

▷   15.2; 27.2 *since* as a conjunction

25.8   Means: **with** and **by**

1   The thief opened the door **with** a key.
2   He got in **by** using a key.

1   We use *with* + noun phrase to talk about means. But ▷ 25.9
2   We use *by* + -ing form.

25.9   Means of transport and communication: **by**

1a   Did you go **by** train or **by** air?
b   We went on foot./We walked.
2   We can let them know **by** telegram.

1a   We use *by* + noun (without *the*) to talk about means of transport, e.g. *by train, by air, by bus, by car, by sea, by boat.* (We can also say *on the train, on the plane, on the bus, on my bike* and *in the car*.)
b   But we say *on foot* or we use the verb *walk*.
2   We also use *by* for means of communication, e.g. *by telegram, by letter, by telephone*.

25.10   Describing: **with** and **in**

1   Police are looking for a tall man **with** fair hair.
It's the house **with** the green door.
2   Who's that woman **in** the red dress?
She had a red dress on/was wearing a red dress.

1   In descriptions *with* means having. *a man with fair hair* = a man who has fair hair.
2   We can use *in* or *have (got) . . . on* to talk about clothes.

25.11   **as** and **like**

1   Trevor is working **as** a disc jockey.
I use this room **as** my office.
2   He talks **like** a disc jockey.
She's just **like** her mother.

1   We use *as* to say what someone's job is or what something is used for.
2   We use *like* to compare two things that are the same or similar in some way.

▷   23.4 *as . . . as*

25.12   Adjective + preposition

I'm **afraid of** the dog.
He's very **different from** his brother.
Are you **ready for** a walk?

Some more examples of adjective + preposition: *bored with, fed up with, fond of, good at, interested in, keen on, tired of, worried about.*

26 Verbs with adverbs and prepositions

26.1 Verbs with adverbs (phrasal verbs)

1 We **went away** for two weeks. We only **came back** yesterday.

2 I'm sure I **wrote down** the address, but I think I **threw away** the piece of paper.

3 The plan didn't **come off**—I'm afraid it **fell through**.

4 Mr Gray doesn't want to **give up** smoking, but he's **cutting down** the number of cigarettes he smokes.

A phrasal verb is a verb + adverb, e.g. *go away*.

1,2 Sometimes the meaning of a phrasal verb is clear from the meaning of the verb and adverb, e.g. *go away, come back, write down, throw away*.

3,4 Sometimes the verb + adverb has a special meaning, e.g. here *come off* (= succeed), *fall through* (= not succeed), *give up* (= stop), *cut down* (= reduce).

1,3 These phrasal verbs have no object.

2,4 These phrasal verbs have an object, e.g. *wrote down the address*.

Some other examples of phrasal verbs: *blow up, call off, carry on, fall down, find out, get up, go away, make up, pick up, put down, put up, set off, sit down, take off, wash up, work out.*

26.2 Phrasal verbs with an object

1 The young people **picked up** the litter.
A lorry **took away** all the bottles.

2 The young people **picked** the litter **up**.
A lorry **took** all the bottles **away**.

3 The young people **picked up** the litter left by the crowd.
A lorry **took away** all the bottles they found.

4 What about the litter? ~
The young people **picked** it **up**.
Who took the bottles? ~ A lorry **took** them **away**.

If the object of a phrasal verb is a noun, the adverb can come

1 before the object or

2 after it.

3 If the object is very long (e.g. *the litter left by the crowd*), then the adverb comes in front of it.

4 If the object is a pronoun, the adverb always comes after it.

26.3   Prepositional verbs

We finally **decided on** a holiday in Morocco.
We had to **wait for** the plane.
Can I **look at** your photos?

A prepositional verb is a verb + preposition, e.g. *decide on*.

Some other examples of prepositional verbs: *agree with, arrive at, ask for, believe in, belong to, deal with, depend on, hope for, insist on, laugh at, listen to, look after, look for, pay for, send for, talk about.*

26.4   Phrasal verbs and prepositional verbs

1   *Phrasal verb*
We **paid back** the money.
We **paid** the money **back**.
The money was **paid back**.

2   *Prepositional verb*
We **paid for** the flat.
The flat was **paid for**.

1   If a phrasal verb has an object, the adverb can come before or after it. ▷ 26.2
We normally stress the adverb.
Some examples of adverbs in phrasal verbs: *about, away, back, by, down, in, off, on, out, over, past, round, through, to, under, up.*

2   A prepositional verb always has an object. The object comes after the preposition. ▷ 26.3
We do not normally stress the preposition.
Some examples of prepositions in prepositional verbs: *about, after, at, for, from, in, into, like, of, off, on, to, with.*

26.5   Phrasal-prepositional verbs

I say we should **do away with** this unfair tax.
Let's hurry up and **get on with** the job.
I hope you won't **go back on** your promise now.
Don't **let** Mr Barnes **in on** our secret!
I'm really **looking forward to** our holiday.
Why do you **put up with** all this noise?
Watch out for cows in the road along here!

A phrasal-prepositional verb is a verb + adverb + preposition, e.g. *do away with.*

27 Conjunctions and other linking words

27.1 Main clauses and sub clauses

Two main clauses

1 I've got a headache, and I feel sick.

*Sub clauses (with **if, when** etc.)*

2 We can go if you like.
   If you like, we can go.
   We'll go when this film's over.
   When this film's over, we'll go.

Reported clauses

3 It said in the paper (that) it finishes at ten.
   It finishes at ten, it said in the paper.

Relative clauses

4 The film that came first was awful.
   'Love in the East', which came first, was awful.

Conjunctions

1 We join two main clauses together with the conjunctions *and, but* and *or*.

2 A sub clause can begin with a conjunction, e.g. *if, when, because, so that*.

3 A reported clause begins with *that* or has no conjunction. ▷ 12.1. For reported questions ▷ 12.5

4 A relative clause begins with a relative pronoun. ▷ 22.1. But ▷ 22.4

Order of clauses

2 A sub clause with *if, when* etc. can come before or after the main clause.

3 A reported clause usually comes after the main clause.

4 A relative clause comes after the noun it tells us about.

Punctuation

For the use of commas with main clauses and sub clauses ▷ 39.3

▷ 13.2 sub clauses of future time

27.2   Clauses of time

When/While/As I was eating my lunch, the fire alarm rang suddenly.
He wanted to have everything ready **before the guests arrived**.
After/When she had wrapped up the parcel, she took it to the post office.
I came **as soon as I heard the news**.
We can wait here **till/until the rain stops**.
We haven't seen Sue **since she came back from her holiday**.

Clauses of time can come either before or after the main clause.

▷ 13.2 sub clauses of future time; 15.2; 17.2 the -ing form

27.3   Sub clauses with **that** and with question words

1   *With* **that**
The problem is (**that**) **we haven't got a key**.
I forgot (**that**) **he was coming today**.
I'm worried (**that**) **you might hurt yourself**.
It seems unlikely (**that**) **the experiment will succeed**.
That the experiment will succeed seems unlikely.

2   *With question words*
I'm trying to find out **when the concert is**.
No one can understand **how the accident happened**.
Sarah wasn't sure **where she'd put the letter**.
What we're going to do about it is the important question.

We can use these sub clauses as subject or object of a sentence, after *be*, or after an adjective.

1   We can leave out *that* in informal English except at the beginning of a sentence.

▷ 12.1 reporting verbs; 20.2 uses of *it*

2   The word order after a question word is the same as in a statement (not a question).

▷ 12.5 reported questions; 28.5 *what* used for emphasis

27.4   Clauses with **and, too, as well** etc.

1   Stephen rides a motor-bike, and he can drive a car (**too/as well**).
Stephen rides a motor-bike. He can drive a car **too/as well**.

2   Jenny can't sing, and she can't dance **either**.
Jenny can't sing. She can't dance **either**.

3   The old man couldn't read **or** write.

4   Stephen rides a motor-bike. He can **also** drive a car.

5   David likes modern jazz **as well as** pop music.
He likes **both** pop music **and** modern jazz.
Jean is **not only** a good singer **but also** a first-class guitarist.

1   *too* and *as well* usually come at the end of a clause.

2   We use *either* instead of *too* in a negative sentence.

3   We normally use *or* instead of *and* to link two words or phrases after a negative.

4   *also* usually has mid position.

5   *as well as, both . . . and* and *not only . . . but also* are more emphatic.

▷   9.1 short additions to statements

27.5   Giving alternatives

1   We can buy a colour television **or** a black and white one.

2   We can buy **either** a colour television **or** a black and white one.
We can **either** buy a television **or** hire one.
There isn't any sport today on BBC **or** on ITV/**either** on BBC **or** on ITV.

3   **Neither** BBC **nor** ITV is/are showing any sport.

1   We use *or* to talk about an alternative.

2   We can use *either* and *or* in a positive or a negative sentence.

3   *neither* and *nor* have a negative meaning.

We use *either* and *neither* to talk about *two* things.
▷ 20.23

▷   8.2 alternative questions

27.6   Clauses of contrast:
whereas, while and **on the other hand**

America is a rich country, **whereas/while** India is a poor country.
America is an industrial country. India, **on the other hand**, is an agricultural country.

on the other hand often has mid position or comes after the subject. It can also have front or end position.

27.7 Clauses of contrast: **but, though, however** etc.

1 Thousands of pupils are leaving school, **but** there are no jobs for them.
  There are no jobs for them, **though**.
  There are, **however**, no jobs for them.

2 **Although/Though/Even though** Ann did well at school, she can't find a job.
  Ann can't find a job **in spite of** doing well at school.

1 As an adverb, *though* usually comes at the end of a sentence. *though* is rather informal.
  however often has mid position or comes after the subject. It can also have front or end position.

2 Clauses with *although, though* and *even though* and with *in spite of* + -ing form can come either before or after the main clause.
  We can also use *in spite of* + noun phrase, e.g. *She can't find a job in spite of her exam results.*

▷   15.2 the -ing form

27.8 Clauses of reason

They didn't go **because** it was snowing.
As/Since we were late, we didn't get any food.

We can express reason with *because, as* or *since*.
We can sometimes use *because of* + noun phrase instead of a clause, e.g. *They didn't go because of the snow.*

▷   17.4 the -ing form and the -ed form

27.9 Clauses of purpose

1 The government puts up taxes **to** get more money from us.
  We need more money **in order to** build more hospitals.
  They called a meeting **so as to** hear everyone's opinion.

2 I wrote down the address **so that** I wouldn't forget it.

3 Schools are **for** learning.

4 What's the meeting **for**? ~
  It's **to** discuss the new plan.

We can express purpose by using

1 an infinitive after *to, in order to* or *so as to. in order to* and *so as to* are rather formal.

2 a clause with *so that*. We often use *can, could, will, would* or *needn't*.

3 *for* + -ing form.

4 We often answer the question *What . . . for?* in a sentence with *to* and the infinitive.

27.10 Clauses of result: **so, therefore** etc.

1 The party wasn't very good, **so** I left early.
2 The management refused to increase wages, and the workers **therefore** went on strike.
3 The club bought two new players, and **as a result** they began to win more games.
   This year's harvest was very poor. **Consequently** the price of wheat has gone up dramatically.

1 (*and*) *so* always comes at the beginning of a clause, but it does not normally start a new sentence.
2 *therefore* often has mid position, but it can have front or end position.
3 *as a result* and *consequently* often have front position but they can have mid or end position.

   We can use *therefore, as a result* and *consequently* in a clause with *and* (e.g. *and as a result* . . .) or in a new sentence (e.g. *Consequently* . . .).

27.11 Clauses of result: **so/such . . . (that) . . .**

We laughed **so** much (**that**) it hurt.
I was **so** tired (**that**) I fell asleep in the taxi.
It was **such** a lovely day (**that**) we simply had to go out somewhere.
Tom talks **such** nonsense (**that**) no one listens to him any more.

We can leave out *that* in informal speech.

27.12 Conditional clauses

We can stop **if** you want.
Even if Marcia leaves now, she'll still be late.
You can't go in **unless** you've got a ticket.
We have to do the job **whether** we like it or not.
You can borrow it **as long as** you give it back.
I don't mind working overtime **provided** (**that**) I'm paid for it.
Take an umbrella **in case** it rains.

These clauses can come before or after the main clause.
unless = if . . . not

▷ 11 if-clauses

28 Emphasis

28.1 Emphatic stress

The party isn't on Saturday—it's on *Friday*.
Will your German friend be there? ~
He's *Dutch* not German.

When we want to give emphasis to a word or phrase (make it more important), we can speak it with extra stress.

In writing we can underline the word to give it emphasis. In a book the word can be printed differently, as in the examples.

28.2 The emphatic form of the verb

1 These motorways aren't necessary. ~
  I think they *are* necessary.
  They shouldn't build them. ~
  I think they *should* build them.
2 People don't use them. ~
  But people *do* use them.
  You didn't come on the motorway. ~
  I *did* come on the motorway.

We use the emphatic form of the verb to give emphasis to the meaning of a whole sentence.

1 Auxiliary and modal verbs are stressed in the emphatic form.
2 The simple present and simple past tenses have an emphatic form with *do*. The form of *do* is stressed. ▷ 5.1

28.3 Emphatic word order

1 '**Eatwell**' the restaurant was called.
2 The steak was nice, but **this pudding** I don't like at all.
3 **Slowly** the restaurant began to fill up.

If we want to give emphasis to a word or phrase, we can put it at the beginning of the clause or sentence. We can do this with

1 a complement
2 an object
3 an adverb

28.4   **it** + **be** used for emphasis

1   **It was your wife** who told us the news.
2   **It was in 1979** that we went to Yugoslavia.
3   **It's Bob** I'm looking for, not Mike.
4   **It wasn't me** that broke the window.

1   We can use *it* + *be* and a relative clause to give emphasis to a noun phrase, e.g. *your wife*.
2   We can also use *it* + *be* to give emphasis to an adverb or adverb phrase, e.g. *in 1979*.
3   We can leave out *who* or *that* when it is the object of the relative clause or when there is a preposition. ▷ 22.4
4   If we use a pronoun after *it* + *be*, we use the object form, e.g. *me*. ▷ 20.1

28.5   **what** used for emphasis

I need a good sleep.
What I need is a good sleep.
I'm going to go to bed.
What I'm going to do is go to bed.

We can use *what* + clause + *be* to give emphasis to a word or phrase, e.g. *a good sleep*.
what = the thing that

▷   22.9 *what* in relative clauses; 27.3 *what* in other sub clauses

28.6   Emphatic use of **here** and **there**

The bus is late. ~ **Here it comes** now, look.
Here comes the bus.
Where are the books? ~ **There they are**.
There are the books, over there.

Form

We can use *here* or *there* to begin a sentence.
The verb is the present tense of *be* or a verb in the simple present tense (usually *come* or *go*).
If the subject is a pronoun, it comes before the verb (e.g. *Here it comes*). If the subject is a phrase with a noun, it comes after the verb (*Here comes the bus*).

Use

We use *here* and *there* at the beginning of a sentence to draw someone's attention to (= make someone look at) something that we can see.

29 Communication:
Starting and finishing a conversation; being friendly

29.1 Starting a conversation with a stranger

Excuse me, could you tell me the time?
I beg your pardon, do you have the time?(*USA*)

29.2 Introductions

Introducing people
Tony, **this is** Elaine.
Pamela, **meet** Andy./**have you met** Andy?/**do you know** Andy?
Mrs Green, **I'd like you to meet/let me introduce you to** Mr Bridges.(*rather formal*)

Meeting someone for the first time
Hello, Andy. ~ **Hello**, Pamela.(*informal*)
Hi, Elaine. ~ **Hi**, Tony.(*informal, and especially USA*)
How do you do? ~ **How do you do?** Pleased to meet you.(*rather formal*)
How are you?~ **How are you?**(*USA*)

29.3 Meeting someone you already know

Greeting someone
Hello, Paul.
Hi, Sue.(*informal and especially USA*)
Good morning./Good afternoon./Good evening.
(*a little more formal than* hello)
Morning./Afternoon./Evening.
(*leaving out* good *is less formal*)

Being polite
Nice to see you. **How are you?** ~
Very well, thank you./ Fine, thanks. And how are you?/And you? ~ **OK, thanks./Not too bad, thanks. How's life?/How are things?**(*informal*)

We use *how* for a polite enquiry but *What . . . like?* for a question about the special qualities of someone or something, e.g. *What's her husband like? ~ Well, he's a rather quiet person.*

29.4   Starting a telephone conversation

Saying who you are and who you are calling
Hello. This is Carl./ Carl **here**./Carl **speaking**.
Can I speak to Maria?/**Is** Maria **there**, please?

Asking who the other person is
Is that Mr Tucker? **Is that** Ashford 73780?
Is this Elaine? (*USA*)
Who's speaking?/**Who am I speaking to**, please?

When you think you have been cut off
Hello? Are you there?

29.5   Saying goodbye

Well, I must be going now./I have to go now. **Goodbye**, Phil.
(I'll) see you (later).
Bye!/Bye-bye! (*informal*)
Cheerio!/So long! (*informal*)
Good night. (*at the end of the day*)

29.6   Starting and finishing a letter

Starting a letter

Informal	Formal
Dear Brian,	**Dear Sir,**
Dear Mrs Moody,	**Dear Madam,**

Finishing a letter

Informal	Formal
Yours sincerely,	**Yours faithfully,**
Sincerely yours, (*USA*)	
Yours (ever),	
Love (from),	

29.7   Good wishes

Good wishes for success
All the best. Good luck in your new job.
I hope everything goes all right/ goes well for you.
I'd like to wish you every success. (*more formal*)

Good wishes to a third person
Remember me to Chris./ **Regards to** Chris./
Love to Chris.

Good wishes for a holiday etc.
Enjoy yourself/yourselves.
Have a good time/holiday/trip/journey.
Look after yourself. Take care on the roads.

Good wishes at special times of the year
Merry Christmas./Happy Christmas. And a
Happy New Year.
Have a nice Easter.
Happy birthday./Many happy returns (of the day).

Before drinking
Cheers! (To your very) good health./Here's to
the two of you.
There is no special phrase spoken before a meal.

29.8   Compliments

Clothes
I like your coat./**That's a lovely** coat./**You look nice in** that coat. ~
Thank you. It's nice of you to say so.

Cooking
That was **a nice/lovely meal.** The steak was **delicious**. ~
I'm glad you enjoyed it.

29.9   Congratulations and sympathy

Congratulations
I hear you've passed your exam. **Well done!**
Congratulations on passing the exam. ~ Thank you.

When someone has been unsuccessful
Bad luck./Hard luck. Never mind. Better luck next time.

Sympathy
My father died last week. ~ Oh, **I am sorry**.
I was very sorry to hear about your father.

30 Communication: Information, opinions and ideas

30.1 Asking for information

Excuse me. **Can you tell me** the way to Oxford Street?
Could you tell me what time the next train to Bristol is, please?
Do you know if there are any seats left?
Could you give me some information about things to do here?

30.2 Agreeing with or correcting a statement

Statement	Agreeing	Correcting
It's the fifth of May today (, isn't it?) ~	**Yes**, it is.	**No**, it isn't; it's the sixth.
	That's right.	It's the sixth **actually**.

30.3 Asking about language

When you don't hear what someone says
Pardon? Could you repeat that, please?
I beg your pardon?
I'm sorry, I didn't catch what you said.

When you don't understand
I'm sorry, **I don't understand**.
What do you mean?
I'm not with you.(*informal*)

Asking the meaning of a word
What's 'cider'? ~ It's a drink made from apples.
What does 'annually' **mean**? ~ It means 'every year'.
What's the meaning of the word 'library'? ~
A library is a place you can borrow books from.

Asking for a word
What do you call it when water becomes ice? ~
We say it 'freezes'.
What's the word for the thing you put a letter in? ~
Oh, you mean an 'envelope'.

Asking about pronunciation and spelling
How do you pronounce this word?
How do you say that?
How do you spell 'sincerely'?
How is it spelt?

30.4   Explanations

Asking for an explanation

Why won't they serve me?
Could you explain why they won't give me a drink?
Could someone **please tell me** what's happening?
I don't understand why we have to go.
I just **don't see** why the pub has to close now.

Giving an explanation

The reason is that it's eleven o'clock.
Well, **the thing is**, pubs can only open till eleven.
It's like this, you see. There's a law which says . . .

Saying that you understand
Oh, I see.
I understand now, thank you.

30.5   Being sure and unsure

Being sure

I'm sure/I'm certain/I know there's a bank in this street.
There**'ll** be one here./ There **must** be one here. ▷ 7.10
There's **certainly/definitely** one in the next street.

Being less sure

It's **probably** that way.
I think/I should think/I believe we have to turn right here.
I don't think/I doubt if we should go left.
I suppose/I expect that's the road to the village.

Being unsure

Maybe/Perhaps we can go straight on.
That **may/might/could** be the road to the village. ▷ 7.7, 8

Not knowing

I don't know/I'm not sure/I've no idea/I wouldn't like to say how far it is to the village.

30.6   Predictions

Brazil **will** win the World Cup. ▷ 4.1
West Germany have a good team. I think they**'re going to** win. ▷ 4.3
I bet/I expect it'll be exciting.
I guess a South American country will win. (*USA*)
The Italians **are sure to** do well/**are bound to** do well.
I'm sure the Italians are going to do well.

30.7 Opinions

Asking for an opinion

What do you think about the strike?
What's your opinion of the workers' action?
Do you agree with/Are you in favour of the
workers getting more money?

▷   35.1 approving and disapproving

Giving an opinion

Well, personally, **I think/I believe/I('d) say/I feel**
they should go back to work.
I don't think they should be on strike.
As far as I can see,/As far as I'm concerned,/It
seems to me/In my opinion, the workers are badly paid.
I'm convinced the workers are right. (*emphatic*)

Agreeing with an opinion
I (quite) agree./That's right./Quite./Exactly./Of course.

Disagreeing with an opinion
I don't agree/I disagree.
I wouldn't say that./I'm not so sure./I wonder./
Do you really think so? (*more polite*)
But **don't you think** . . .?/Well, **I think** . . ./But **on**
the other hand . . ./**Yes, but** . . .

30.8 Having ideas

Just **imagine** if there was life on Mars.
What if the people there could build spaceships?
Supposing they visited the earth?
I wonder what I'd say to a person from Mars.

▷   7.9 *would*; 13.3 the unreal present

31 Communication: Telling and asking people to do things

31.1 Orders

Open your mouth, please. **Don't** talk. ▷ 6.1
You **must** sleep now. You **mustn't** talk. ▷ 7.4
You**'re to** drink this. You**'re not to** leave any.
I want you to drink it all. ▷ 14.6
Fasten seat belts. **No** smoking. (*written*)
Ball games are **prohibited**. (*written*)
Nurses **will** wear uniform at all times. (*a strict order*)

Ordering food and drink
I'll have the chicken.
A coke **for me**, please.

Sometimes we put an order in the form of a request
(▷ 31.2) to make it more polite,
e.g. *Could you open your mouth, please?*

31.2 Requests

Making a request
Would you mind taking me to the station?
Would you like to wash up?
Would you pass the butter, please?
Will you wait a moment, please?
Could you tell me when the next train is?
Can I have some water, please?
Open the window, **would you?/will you?/could
you?/can you?** (*informal*)
Passengers **are requested to** remain in their
seats. (*formal*)

would you mind + *-ing* form is a polite request.
would and *could* are rather more polite than
will and *can*.

▷ 11.2 if-clauses

Asking someone to move out of the way
Excuse me. Can I get past?

Agreeing to a request
**OK./All right./Yes, of course./Sure.
Certainly.** (*more formal*)

Refusing a request
Unfortunately I haven't time.
I have to go now, **actually**.
I'm sorry, but I'm just going out.
I'm afraid I can't just at the moment.

31.3   Permission

Asking permission

Can I use your pen?
May I borrow this book, please?
(*more formal than* Can I . . .?)
Do you mind if I open the window?
Is it all right if we sit here?

Giving permission

Yes, **of course.** Go ahead.
Of course **you can/you may**.
Yes, **all right**.
Certainly. (*more formal*)

Refusing permission

No, **I'm afraid** that's not possible.
I'm sorry, I'm reading it myself at
the moment.

▷   7.3 *can, may, be allowed to*

31.4   Suggestions

Asking for a suggestion

What **shall/can** we do?
Have you got any ideas/suggestions?

Making a suggestion

Shall we go for a swim?
What about/How about playing cards/
a game of cards?
Why don't we/**Why not** lie in the sun?
Let's go for a walk (, **shall we**?) ▷ 6.2
We **could** go to the park. ▷ 7.8

Agreeing with a suggestion

Good idea./OK./Fine./Yes, let's do that./Yes, why not?

Disagreeing with a suggestion

Well, **I was just going to** make some coffee.
I don't feel like cards/don't want to play cards, **actually**.
I'm sorry, it's too hot for me. Let's go to the club **instead**.
That would be nice, but I have to meet someone.

31.5   Advice

Asking for advice

What **shall** I do?
What **should** I do/**ought** I **to** do about
a job? ▷ 7.6
What **would** you do **in my position?/
if you were me?** ▷ 7.9
Could you advise me what to do?
I'd like to ask your advice about a job.

Giving advice

I think you **ought to/should/had better** talk to your parents.
If I were you,/If you ask me, I wouldn't leave school yet.
Well, **I'd advise you to** stay at school.
If you want/ask/take my advice, you won't decide in a hurry.
The best thing for you to do is talk to your head teacher.

31.6   Telling someone how to do something

Turn left and then **take** the first turning on the right.
Don't touch it until it's dry.
First you beat the eggs, **and then** you have to
add some sugar.

When you've done that, you . . .
Make sure it's clean.
You **must** pull hard.
This is how you do it./You do it like this.

31.7   Warnings

Look out!/Watch out! (*warning of immediate danger*)
If you take all those glasses, you**'ll** drop them. ▷ 11.1
They're heavy, **I'm warning you./I warn you./
let me warn you.**

Mind those glasses.
Be careful, or there'll be an accident..

31.8   Reminders

Don't forget your money./**Don't forget to** take your money.
Remember to post the letter.
Make sure you lock the door.

31.9   Threats

Don't move **or I'll** shoot!
If you do anything stupid **you'll** be sorry.

Any trouble from you **and I'll** call the police.

31.10   Insisting

I really must have the money today.
I'm sorry to insist, but I need it today.
I'm afraid I **simply can't** wait any longer.

It's absolutely essential you pay me today.
I insist on having it now. (*formal*)

31.11   Persuading

Why don't you join the club? ~ I don't want to.
Why not? All your friends go there.
Go on./Come on. You could try it. You might enjoy
it. ~ Well, I don't know. I'll think about it.

Look, it would be better than doing nothing,
wouldn't it? You **really must** get out sometimes. ~
Oh, all right then. I'll go next week.

32 Communication: Decisions and intentions

32.1 Decisions

Asking someone to decide
What **are you going to** do?
Have you decided/Have you made up your mind
where you'd like to go this evening?

Making a decision
Yes, **I'll** buy it.
I think I'll go home now.

Changing a decision
I've changed my mind. I want
this one instead.

32.2 Intentions

I'm going to visit the USA next year. ▷ 4.3
I've decided to go there/**I've decided on** the USA.
I intend to see as much as I can.

I may go/**I might** go/**I'm thinking of** going to
Los Angeles. (*less sure*) ▷ 7.7

32.3 Willingness

Asking if someone is willing
Are you willing to/prepared to work on Sundays?
Would you be willing to/prepared to organize the competition?
Do you mind/Would you mind sleeping on the sofa?

Saying you are willing
I'm perfectly **willing** to help.
I'd be prepared to wait a day or two.
I don't mind/I wouldn't mind walking.

Saying you are unwilling
I'm not prepared to go to so much trouble.
I wouldn't be willing to do anything dangerous.

32.4 Refusing

I won't put up with rudeness.
I'm not going to pay £1 to go in.

I refuse to wait any longer.
I'm afraid **it's quite out of the question**. (*formal*)

No way! (*informal*)

32.5 Promises

You**'ll**/ You **will**/You **shall** get your money back.
I**'ll**/I **will**/I **shall** give it you back by the weekend.

I promise I'll do it/**I promise to** do it tomorrow.
I won't be long, **I promise.**

33 Communication: Offers and invitations

33.1 Offers

Offering to help

Let me help you.
Can I carry that suitcase?
I'll take this bag, (**shall I?**)
Shall I do it for you?
Would you like me to get you a taxi?

Offering e.g. food or drink

Would you like/Will you have/Won't you have something to eat?
(Do) have some tea. (*informal*)

Accepting an offer

Yes, please. **Thank you** very much. That's very kind of you.

Refusing an offer

(*of help*) **No, thank you**. It's all right. I can manage.
(*of food or drink*) **No, thank you./Not just now, thank you**.

33.2 Invitations

Giving an invitation

Would you like to have dinner with us?
Will you have/**Won't you** have dinner with us?
(Do) come and see us tomorrow. (*informal*)
What about coming/**How about** coming to our house? (*informal*)
Do you feel like coming/**Do you want to** come to a party? (*informal*)

Accepting an invitation

That's very nice of you. **Thank you./Yes, fine**. I'll look forward to it.
Yes, **that'd be nice/lovely**. I'd be delighted to come.

Refusing an invitation

Well, **that's very kind of you, but** I won't be here tomorrow.
I'd love to, but I'm afraid I have some work to do.
Well, **thank you very much, but** I'm afraid I can't.
I'm afraid I won't be here, **but thank you all the same**.

33.3 Thanks

Thanking someone

Thanks./Thanks a lot./Thanks very much. (*informal*)
Thank you./Thank you very much.
That's very good/kind/nice of you. **Thank you very much indeed**. I'm very grateful to you. (*emphatic*)

Answering someone who thanks you

That's all right/OK.
It's a pleasure./Not at all./Don't mention it.
You're welcome. (*mostly USA*)

There is often no answer after *thank you* etc. in British English.

34 Communication: Feelings

34.1 Exclamations

how + *adjective*

Someone broke into the house while we were away. ~
Oh, **how** awful!
How funny that programme was!

what + *noun phrase*

What a lovely view you've got from your house!
What nonsense!
Oh, **what** beautiful flowers!

Negative question forms

Isn't it lovely!
Wasn't that fun!

Other types of exclamation

Help!
Hey, you!
Oh, well done!

34.2 Being pleased and annoyed

Being pleased

I've won £1000. ~ That's **good/great**.
That's **wonderful/marvellous/terrific**. (*more emphatic*)

Being annoyed

The train is half an hour late. ~
Oh, no!/Oh, dear. What a nuisance!
Oh, hell!/Damn! (*swear words*)

34.3 Likes and dislikes

Asking about likes

Do you like that colour?
How do you like this picture?
What did you think of the film?

Expressing likes

This place is **nice/great/lovely**, isn't it?
I like/I love/I enjoy/I'm fond of the seaside.
I like/I love/I enjoy/I'm fond of going to parties.
It's my **favourite** drink.

Expressing dislikes

This programme's **not very good/not very interesting.**
It's **terrible/awful**.(*more emphatic*)
I don't like/I dislike/I hate pop music.
I don't like/I dislike/I hate doing the cleaning.
I can't bear/I can't stand that man. (*more emphatic*)
I can't bear to sit and do nothing.
I'm fed up with this programme/with watching this rubbish.

▷   16.2 the infinitive and the -ing form

34.4   Looking forward to something

With pleasure
I'm really **looking forward to** my holiday./**to** going away.
I can't wait to get on the plane.

Without pleasure
I'm not looking forward to the exam at all.
I'm dreading next Thursday.

34.5   Wishing and hoping

Wishing
I wish the weather was nicer./it would stop raining.
If only something exciting would happen.
Why can't/won't these flies go away?
I'd like to/I'd love to/I want to have a holiday right now.
I'm dying to sit down. **I'm dying for** a drink.(*more emphatic*)

Hoping
I hope the parcel comes soon.
Let's hope it hasn't got lost.

▷   13.3 the unreal present

34.6   Preferences

Asking about preferences
Would you prefer/Do you prefer tea or coffee?
Would you rather have milk or cream?
Which would you like?

Expressing preference
I'd prefer to go out rather than sit here.
I usually **prefer** walking **to** doing nothing./**like** walking **better than** doing nothing.
I'd rather do something **than** just sit. **I'd rather not** stay here.
I'd rather you came with me. ▷ 13.3

Having no preference
I don't mind/I don't care what we do. It's all the same to me.
It doesn't matter to me where we go.

34.7   Showing surprise and interest

Surprise
I'm going to give up my job. ~ You're not, are you? ▷ 8.5
Are you **really**? ▷ 9.1
Really? Well, **that** *is* **a surprise**.
Good heavens./Good Lord.
You aren't going to sell the house, are you? ▷ 8.5
Aren't you going to work here any more? ▷ 8.3

Interest
I'm going to buy a farm. ~ Oh, are you? ▷ 9.1
Oh, **really**? **That** *is* **interesting**.
So you're going to buy a farm, are you? ▷ 8.5

34.8   Regret

Unfortunately/I'm afraid the car won't start.
What a pity!/shame!
It's a pity/shame it happened today.
I'm sorry to say/**I regret** to say we're going to miss the show.
I'm sorry not to have seen/**I regret** not having seen the show.
(regret *is more formal*)

34.9   Worry

Asking someone what the matter is
What's the matter?/What's wrong?/What's up?
(Is) anything wrong/the matter?

Being worried
I'm worried about the money.

Telling someone not to worry
Don't worry./There's nothing to worry about.
It's all right./It's OK./It doesn't matter.

Expressing relief
I've found the passport. ~ Oh, **thank goodness** for that. That's a relief.
Thank goodness we caught the train.

35 Communication: Right and wrong

35.1 Approving and disapproving

Approving

I'm glad/I'm pleased the government are increasing the tax on petrol.
The government are **right**/It's **right** to do it.
They're **doing the right thing. It's a good idea.**
I approve of them making petrol more expensive.
I'm in favour of it. **I'm all for it.**(*informal*)

▷   30.7 opinions

Disapproving

People **oughtn't to** drive/**shouldn't** drive big cars.▷ 7.6
It's **wrong/not right** to use so much petrol.
I don't approve of/**I disapprove** of people using up so much energy.
I'm against people driving big cars.

35.2 Blaming someone

The accident was the lorry driver**'s fault**.
I blame the lorry driver. The lorry driver was **to blame**.
He **ought to have/should have** stopped.▷ 7.6, 15

35.3 Complaining

I'm afraid I have a complaint to make about the food.
I'm sorry to have to say this, but the service isn't very good.
Look, **I really must protest** about the condition of my room.
Can't something be done to stop the noise?

35.4 Apologies

Making an apology

I'm sorry I've damaged your car.
I'm very/extremely/awfully/terribly sorry.
I beg your pardon.
I apologize/I do apologize▷ 28.2
Please accept my apologies(*formal*)
Excuse me./Pardon me(*starting or interrupting a conversation; after sneezing, coughing etc.*)

Accepting an apology

That's all right/OK, as long as you pay for the damage.
It doesn't matter.
Don't worry. Forget it(*informal*)

36 Numbers, money etc.

36.1 Cardinal numbers

0 nought/zero/oh

1 one	11 **eleven**	21 twenty-one
2 two	12 **twelve**	22 twenty-two
3 three	13 **thir**teen	30 **thir**ty
4 four	14 fourteen	40 **for**ty
5 five	15 **fif**teen	50 **fif**ty
6 six	16 sixteen	60 sixty
7 seven	17 seventeen	70 seventy
8 eight	18 eighteen	80 eighty
9 nine	19 nineteen	90 ninety
10 ten	20 **twen**ty	100 a/one hundred

101	a/one hundred and one
138	a/one hundred and thirty-eight
572	five hundred and seventy-two
1,000	a/one thousand
36,429	thirty-six thousand four hundred and twenty-nine
1,000,000	a/one million

In British English *and* comes between the hundreds and the rest of the number e.g. *five hundred and seventy-two*. But Americans say *five hundred seventy-two* without *and*.

In informal English we can say *a hundred* or *a thousand* etc. instead of *one hundred* or *one thousand*, but only at the beginning of a number.

hundred, thousand. million etc. do not have *-s* except in indefinite numbers, e.g. *There were thousands of people in the stadium*.

one thousand is written 1,000 or 1000.

In British English *a billion* usually means one thousand million, but it can mean one million million.

We usually speak the number 0 as *nought* (mainly GB) or *zero* (mainly USA). ▷ 36.6

In telephone numbers we say *oh*. ▷ 36.9

For *a/an* and *one* ▷ 19.2

36.2 **exactly, about, over** etc.

I've got **exactly** £12.69 on me.
(= £12.69, no more and no less)

I've read **about** fifty pages of the book.
(= not exactly fifty, perhaps between forty and sixty)

We've had this washing-machine **over** ten years/**more than** ten years now.
(= perhaps eleven or twelve years)

The job will take **at least** five days.
(= five days or more)

He earns **under** £100/**less than** £100 a week.
(= perhaps £90 or £95)

There are **almost/nearly** 4 million people without a job in this country.
(= only a few less than 4 million, perhaps 3,900,000)

36.3   Ordinal numbers

1st	**first**	11th	eleventh
2nd	**second**	12th	**twelf**th
3rd	**third**	13th	thirteenth
		20th	twent**ieth**
4th	fourth	40th	fort**ieth**
5th	**fif**th	50th	fift**ieth**
8th	eighth	86th	eighty-sixth
9th	**nin**th	90th	ninet**ieth**
10th	**tenth**	100th	hundredth/one hundredth

101st   (one) hundred and **first**
133rd   (one) hundred and thirty-**third**
157th   (one) hundred and fifty-seventh
1,000th   (one) thousandth

The British runner David Barton came **tenth** in the race.
They've already got five children, and she's expecting a **sixth**.
The washing-machine has broken down for the **third** time this year.
Today's programme is the (**one**) **hundred and seventy-eighth** in the series.
Elizabeth II ('Elizabeth the second').

▷   36.5 fractions; 36.11 dates

36.4   **once, twice** etc.

I clean my teeth **once** a day/**twice** a day/**three times** a day/**four times** a day.

We use *once, twice* etc. to express frequency.
▷ 24.7
We use *times* with numbers above *two*.

36.5   Fractions

½	a/one **half**	half an hour ▷ 20.23
⅓	a/one **third**	a third of a mile
¾	three **quarters**	three quarters of a pound
⅝	five **eighths**	five eighths of an inch
1½	one and a half	one and a half days/ a day and a half

3⅔ three and two thirds   three and two third metres
5¼ five and a quarter   five and a quarter hours
³³⁄₇₆ thirty-three over seventy-six *or* thirty-three seventy sixths

36.6   Decimals

0·5	point five/nought point five zero point five (*USA*) (= ½)
2·33	two point three three (= 2⅓)

5·75 five point seven five (= 5¾)
6·08 six point oh eight

36.7 Percentages

50% fifty **per cent** [pə'sent]   2½% two and a half **per cent**   6·25% six point two five **per cent**

36.8 Sums

16 + 7 = 23   Sixteen **and** seven **is** twenty-three.
Sixteen **plus** seven **equals** twenty-three.
18 − 5 = 13   Eighteen **take away** five **is** thirteen.
Eighteen **minus** five **equals** thirteen.
  4 × 9 = 36   Four nines **are** thirty-six.
Four **times** nine **is** thirty-six.
Four **multiplied by** nine **equals** thirty-six.
27 ÷ 3 = 9   Twenty-seven **divided by** three **is/equals** nine.

36.9 Telephone numbers

Telephone 0270 53399   oh two seven oh, five three three nine nine
oh two seven oh, five double three double nine

36.10 Money

1p	a **penny**/one **p** [pi:]	1¢	a/one **cent**
10p	ten **pence**/ ten **p**	$1	a/one **dollar**
£1	a **pound**/one **pound**	$3·75	three (**dollars**) seventy-five (**cents**)
£3−75 or £3·75	three **pound**(**s**) seventy-five **pence**		
	three **pounds**(**s**) seventy-five		
	three seventy-five		

36.11 Dates

23 June/23rd June   the twenty-third of June
twenty-third June (*USA*)
June 23rd/June 23   June the twenty-third
June twenty-third (*USA*)
1983   nineteen eighty-three

In Britain 1.4.83 = 1st April 1983.
In America 1.4.83 = 4th January 1983.

36.12   The time of day

1	7.00	seven o'clock seven (*informal*)
2	8.00 a.m.	eight a.m. [eɪˈem]/eight o'clock in the morning
	10.00 p.m.	ten p.m. [piːˈem]/ten o'clock in the evening
3	7.30	half past seven/seven thirty half seven (*informal*)
	7.15	(a) quarter past seven/seven fifteen
	7.45	(a) quarter to eight/seven forty-five
	9.20	twenty (minutes) past nine/nine twenty
	9.55	five (minutes) to ten/nine fifty-five
	10.23	twenty-three minutes past ten/ten twenty-three
	10.46	fourteen minutes to eleven/ten forty-six
4	16.08	sixteen oh eight
	21.00	twenty-one (hundred) hours

1   We only use *o'clock* on the hour. We can leave it out in informal speech, e.g. *I'll see you at seven.*

2   We use *a.m.* (= before noon) and *p.m.* (= after noon) or *in the morning/in the afternoon/in the evening/at night* to make clear which part of the day we mean.

3   We normally use *half past seven, five to ten* etc. in informal English. We use *seven thirty, nine fifty-five* etc. to talk about a timetable.

We can leave out *minutes* only after 5, 10, 20 and 25, e.g. *twenty past nine* but *twenty-one minutes past nine*.

after and *of* are also used in American English instead of *past* and *to*, e.g. *twenty after nine, a quarter of eight.*

4   The 24-hour clock is used in timetables. For times on the hour we sometimes say *hundred hours.*

36.13   Measurements

I need a piece of wood about an eighth of an **inch** (⅛")/three **millimetres** (3 mm) thick.
Kay is five **feet** six **inches** (5 ft 6 ins/5′6″)/a hundred and sixty-eight **centimetres** (168 cm) tall.
A **metre** (1 m) is longer than a **yard** (1 yd).
It's five **miles**/eight **kilometres** (8 km) to Bath.
I need four **ounces** (4 oz)/a hundred **grams** (100 gm) of flour.
Four **pounds** (4 lbs)/two **kilos** (2 kg) of potatoes.
I weigh ten **stone** three (10 st 3 lbs)/a hundred forty-three **pounds** (*USA*)/sixty-five **kilos**.
Ben drank a **pint**/half a **litre** of beer with the meal.
We bought five **gallons**/twenty **litres** of petrol.
The temperature is fifty **degrees Fahrenheit** (50°F)/ten **degrees Celsius/Centigrade** (10°C).

1 inch = 25·4 mm
1 inch = 2·54 cm
12 inches = 1 foot = 30·48 cm
3 feet = 1 yard = 91·44 cm
1760 yards = 1 mile = 1·61 km
1 ounce = 28·35 gm
16 ounces = 1 pound = 0·454 kg
14 lbs = 1 stone = 6·356 kg
1 pint = 0·57 litres = 1·20 pints (*USA*)
8 pints = 1 gallon = 4·54 litres = 1·20 gallons (*USA*)

37 Word-building

37.1 Nouns for jobs and other activities

-er/-or

teach**er**, build**er**, wait**er**, manag**er**, driv**er**
doct**or**, edit**or**, act**or**

-ist

art**ist**, chem**ist**, journal**ist**, tour**ist**

-ant/-ent

shop assist**ant**, civil serv**ant**, account**ant**
travel ag**ent**, stud**ent**, presid**ent**

-man/-woman/-person

police**man**, post**man**, milk**man**, sales**man**,
chair**man**
police**woman**, post**woman**
sales**person** (= salesman/saleswoman)
chair**person**

-ess

actr**ess**, waitr**ess**, princ**ess**

There are no rules to say which words have *-er* or
-or or *-ist* etc. You have to look in a dictionary.

Words in *-man* refer to men; words in *-woman* or
-ess refer to women; other words refer to both men
and women, e.g. *teacher, doctor, student*. But we
can say, e.g. *a woman teacher, women doctors, a
male nurse, a female student.*

37.2 Using two nouns together

a **shoe shop**	= a shop that sells shoes
a **bus-driver**	= a person who drives a bus
a **London theatre**	= a theatre in London
a **bedroom**	= a room with a bed
a **stone wall**	= a wall made of stone
an **egg sandwich**	= a sandwich with egg in it
the **river bank**	= the bank of the river

We often use a noun like an adjective by putting it
in front of another noun.

Sometimes the two nouns are written as one
compound word or with a hyphen. ▷ 39.7

The first noun is nearly always singular, e.g.
a shoe shop (a shop that sells shoes).

Some more examples: *police-car, bicycle factory,
youth club, pocket-money, school bus, bank
robber, film star, Christmas present, January
sales, evening meal, housework, paper bag, gold
watch, orange juice, garden gate, table leg,
kitchen door, girl-friend.*

For e.g. *the bank of the river* ▷ 18.7

37.3   Compound nouns with adjective and -ing form

I grow tomatoes in the **greenhouse**.
We sat in the **waiting room**.

greenhouse and *waiting room* are compound nouns. The stress is on the first part of the compound ('greenhouse, 'waiting room).

Some other examples: *high school, grandfather, shorthand, hot dog, drinking water, riding lesson, playing-field, washing-machine, shopping bag.*

For e.g. *the waiting 'car* ▷ 17.1

37.4   Nouns formed from verbs

1   *give* → **giving**, *make* → **making** *etc.*
The **building** of the new university will begin next month.

2   *Same word for verb and noun*
(**attack, change** *etc.*)
The **promise** of more money for schools has pleased teachers.

3   *communicate* → **communication,** *suggest* →
suggestion, *produce* → **production** *etc.*
The **discussion** of our economic problems was very interesting.

4   *move* → **movement,** *develop* → **development**
etc.
The **employment** of 3,000 people will be a great help to the area.

Most nouns formed from verbs have *of* before the object (e.g. *the building of the new university*), but some nouns have other prepositions after them, e.g. *an attack on the government, a change in/of policy.*

37.5   Compound verbal nouns

One of his hobbies is **stamp-collecting**.
Letter-writing is a job I don't enjoy.
I like **sunbathing.**
Is **water-skiing** difficult?

The noun in the compound is always singular, e.g. *stamp-collecting* (= collecting stamps).
We use a hyphen in most of these compounds.

▷   15.1 the -ing form; 37.6 compound adjectives

37.6   Compound adjectives with **-ing** and **-ed**

Noun/adverb + -ing form
Britain is an **oil-producing** country.
Reducing taxes is a **vote-winning** policy.
Are the British **hard-working** enough?

Adverb/adjective + -ed form
Mrs Johnson always looks **well dressed**.
She's the **fair-haired** woman, isn't she?
You've got a very **badly paid** job.

The noun in the compound is always singular, e.g.
a vote-winning policy (= a policy that wins votes).
We normally use a hyphen in a compound adjective, especially when it comes before a noun.

▷   17.1 the -ing form and the -ed form used as adjectives

37.7   Compound adjectives with numbers

Number + noun
They're a **two-car** family.
It's a **fifteen-minute** drive to Glasgow.

Number + noun + adjective
Mr Gould is a **forty-year-old** businessman.
There was a **three-foot-deep** hole in the road.

The noun in the compound is always singular, e.g.
a two-car family (= a family with two cars).
We normally use a hyphen (-) in compound adjectives.
We can only use a compound adjective with a number before a noun. Compare *Mr Gould is forty years old*.
For *fifteen minutes' drive* ▷ 18.6

37.8   Prefixes

1   The story is **untrue**.
It was a very **informal** meeting.
I **disagree** with you.
Let's find a **non-smoker**.

2   Most workers here are **underpaid**.
You can **re-use** these envelopes.
I must have **miscounted** the money.
Those were **pre-war** days.
These shoes are **substandard**.
The government is **pro-Catholic**.
Try the **multi-storey** car park.
We all sat in a **semi-circle**.

We use a prefix to change or add to the meaning of a word. Here are a few examples.

1   We can sometimes use *un-, in-, im-, ir-, il-, dis-* or *non-* to make an opposite. You have to look in a dictionary to find the correct prefix.

2   *under* = not enough   *sub* = below
re = again   *pro* = on the side of
mis = wrongly   *multi* = many
pre = before   *semi* = half

38 The pronunciation and spelling of endings

38.1 The pronunciation of **-s/-es**

1 shops [**ps**] 2 sees [**i:z**] 3 prices [**sɪz**]
  writes [**ts**]   eyes [**aɪz**]   loses [**zɪz**]
  Mick's [**ks**]   jobs [**bz**]   watches [**tʃɪz**]
  cliffs [**fs**]   beds [**dz**]   Mr Blish's [**ʃɪz**]

1 -s is [**s**] after voiceless sounds (but see note 3).
2 -s is [**z**] after voiced sounds (but see note 3).
3 -s/-es is [**ɪz**] after the sounds [**s**], [**z**], [**ʃ**], [**ʒ**], [**tʃ**] and [**dʒ**].

▷ 2.4 the simple present; 18.1, 2 plurals of nouns; 18.4 the possessive form

38.2 Putting in **e** before **-s**

1 dish → dish**es** 2 price → prices
  box → box**es**   lose → loses
  watch → watch**es**   realize → realizes

1 After the sounds [**s**], [**z**], [**ʃ**], [**ʒ**], [**tʃ**] and [**dʒ**] the ending is -es.
2 If the word ends in e, the ending is -s.

38.3 Leaving out **e**

1 writ**e** → writing   3 make → makes
  lik**e** → liked   nice → nicely
  nic**e** → nicer   4 tru**e** → truly
  fin**e** → finest   whol**e** → wholly
2 agr**ee** → agreeing/   5 possibl**e** → possibly
      agreed   probabl**e** → probably

1 We leave out e before an ending with a vowel, e.g. -ing, -ed, -er, -est.
2 If the e is part of a vowel sound (e.g. agree), we do not leave it out before -ing.
3 We do not leave out e before an ending with a consonant, e.g. -s, -ly.
4 But we leave out e from true and whole before -ly.
5 When an adjective ending in -le becomes an adverb, e changes to y.

38.4 The pronunciation of **-ed**

1 stopped [**pt**] 2 showed [**əʊd**] 3 waited [**tɪd**]
  looked [**kt**]   played [**eɪd**]   ended [**dɪd**]
  passed [**st**]   cleaned [**nd**]
  laughed [**ft**]   used [**zd**]

1 -ed is [**t**] after voiceless sounds (but see note 3).
2 -ed is [**d**] after voiced sounds (but see note 3).
3 -ed is [**ɪd**] after [**t**] and [**d**].

38.5   The doubling of consonants

1   plan   pla**nn**ing
    stop   sto**pp**ed
    big   bi**gg**er
    fat   fa**tt**est
2   play   playing
    show   showed
    clean   cleaner
    short   shortest
3   be'gin   begi**nn**ing
4   'visit   visiting
5   travel   trave**ll**ing

1   In short words with one written vowel (*a, e, i, o, u*) + one written consonant (*n, p, g, t* etc.), we double the consonant (*nn, pp, gg, tt*) before an ending with a vowel, e.g. *-ing*, *-ed*, *-er*, or *-est*.
2   We do not double the consonant if it is *y* or *w* (e.g. *play, show*).
    We do not double it if we write the vowel with two letters (e.g. *clean*).
    We do not double it if the word ends in two written consonants (e.g. *short*) or in *x*.
3   In longer words we double the consonant if the last part of the word is stressed (e.g. *be'gin*).
4   We do not double the consonant if the last part of the word is unstressed (e.g. *'visit*).
5   But we double *l* in British English (e.g. GB *travelled*, USA *traveled*).

38.6   Consonant + **y**

1   lady → lad**ie**s
    fly → fl**ie**s
    carry → carr**ie**d
    funny → funn**ie**r
    silly → sill**ie**st
    happy → happ**i**ly.
2   the secretar**y's** desk
    the secretar**ies'** desks
3   play → played
4   fly → fl**y**ing
5   lie → l**y**ing

1   In words ending in a consonant (*d, l, r, n, p* etc.) + *y*, the *y* changes to *ie* before *-s* and to *i* before *-ed, -er, -est* and *-ly*.
2   In the possessive form we use an apostrophe + *s* with a singular noun and an apostrophe with a plural noun. ▷ 18.4
3   *y* does not change after a vowel.
4   *y* does not change before *-ing*.
5   *ie* changes to *y* before *-ing*.

39 Punctuation

39.1 The sentence

1 **W**e'll go for a walk now.
   But bring your coat.

2 **D**o you want to go to **H**yde **P**ark?
   Shall we look at the shops first?
   Are they open on **S**aturdays?

3 **L**ook what **I**'ve got!
   What a fantastic dress!

At the end of a sentence we put

1 a full stop (.) after a statement or imperative
2 a question mark (?) after a question
3 an exclamation mark (!) after an exclamation

We write a capital letter (a big letter)

1 at the beginning of a sentence (e.g. *We . . .* or *But . . .*)
2 at the beginning of each word in a name (e.g. *Hyde Park*) and days and months (e.g. *Saturday*), but not in other nouns (e.g. *shops*)
3 for the word *I*

39.2 The semi-colon

The farmer and his sons start work at six o'clock every morning; they have to get up early because there is always so much to do.

We use a semi-colon (;) between two main clauses when the second main clause is not linked grammatically to the first.

39.3 The comma

We use a comma to show a shorter pause than a semi-colon (;) or a full stop (.). The rules about commas aren't very definite. We can often choose whether to put a comma or not.

1 He looked for the key, but he couldn't find it.
   He looked for the key but couldn't find it.
2a When I saw the photo, I laughed.
 b The questions were easy, Alan said.
 c Mr Sims, who lives opposite, is ninety-six.

We put a comma

1 usually between two main clauses before *but, and* or *or*, but only if the second clause has a subject (e.g. *he*)
2a after a sub clause
 b after a reported clause
 c around a non-defining relative clause ▷ 22.12

d   I laughed when I saw the photo.
e   Alan said (that) the questions were easy.
f   We all saw what happened.
g   The man who lives opposite is ninety-six.
3   The police came to the house to ask him some questions.
4   On Thursday afternoon, they all went out together. They all went out together on Thursday afternoon.
5   Mr Reid, the owner of the company, lives near Southport.
6a The food, however, was good.
b   On the other hand, we need a quick decision.
    We could go to Tunisia, for example.
    Actually, I'm a Liberal.
    It won't be easy, of course.
c   Have you got the number, please? ~ Yes, I have.
7   Have you seen this, Pat?
    Dear Mr Bright,
        Thank you for your letter . . .
8   Inside the room there was a table, two chairs, a lamp and a television set.

d   not usually before a sub clause
e   not before a reported clause
f   not before a question word or *that* ▷ 27.3
g   not with a defining relative clause ▷ 22.12
3   not before an infinitive
4   sometimes after an adverb phrase but not usually before it
5   usually around a phrase in apposition ▷ 18.16
6a usually around a linking word
b   usually after or before a linking word or sentence adverb
c   usually before *please* and after *yes* or *no*
7   before or after the name of a person we are speaking or writing to ▷ 29.6
8   in a list of more than two things

39.4   Quotation marks

David said, 'It's time to go now.'
'It's time to go now,' David said./said David.

We use quotation marks ('. . .') before and after direct speech. We usually put a comma before or after the direct speech.

39.5   The apostrophe

1   These are my girl-friend's records.
2   Chris isn't thirty. He's only twenty-five.

We use the apostrophe
1   in the possessive form of nouns ▷ 18.4
2   in short forms ▷ 39.6

39.6   Short forms

1   We**'ve** had nice weather.
2   This salad**'s** nice.
3   What**'ll** you do?
4   There**'d** be plenty.
5   Here**'s** Sarah now.
6   They are**n't** ready.

Form

When we use the short form, we leave out part of the word we are writing. We put an apostrophe (') instead of the missing part and we write the two words together as one.

Short forms

'm	= am	**'ve**	= have	**won't**	= will not
're	= are	**'d**	= had/would	**n't**	= not
's	= is/has	**'ll**	= will/shall		

Sometimes there are alternative short forms, e.g.
it is not → it isn't/it's not
they will not → they won't/they'll not

Use

We can use a short form only if the word is unstressed. We do not use short forms in short answers with *yes* (*Yes, we have*) or when a word is stressed (*We really 'have had nice weather*).

We can use short forms

1   after a pronoun
2   sometimes after a noun
3   sometimes after a question word
4   after *there* and *that*
5   for *is* after *here*
6   for *not* after an auxiliary or modal verb

We use short forms when we write down an informal conversation or in informal writing, e.g. in a letter or a postcard to a friend.

39.7   The hyphen

1a   That's a **police dog**.
b   I've rung the **police-station**.
c   Here's a **policeman**.
2   There's a **three-mile-long** tunnel.
3   Don't **over-fill** the tank.
     We can **re-use** these bottles.

1   The rules about hyphens aren't very definite. We write some compound nouns as two words (a), some with a hyphen (b) and some as one word (c).
2   We normally use a hyphen in compound adjectives. ▷ 37.6, 7
3   We often use a hyphen after a prefix. ▷ 37.8

40 List of common irregular verbs

Base form*	Past tense	Past participle	Base form*	Past tense	Past participle	Base form*	Past tense	Past participle
awake	awoke	awaked/awoke	forgive	forgave	forgiven	set	set	set
be (am, is, are)	was, were	been	freeze	froze	frozen	shake	shook	shaken
beat	beat	beaten	get	got	got/gotten (USA)	shine [aɪ]	shone [ɒ]	shone [ɒ]
become	became	become	give	gave	given	shoot	shot	shot
begin	began	begun	go (goes)	went	gone ▷ 5.4	show	showed	shown/showed
bend	bent	bent	grow	grew	grown	shut	shut	shut
bet	bet/betted	bet	hang	hung	hung	sing	sang	sung
bite	bit	bitten/bit	have (has)	had	had	sink	sank	sunk
blow	blew	blown	hear [ɪə]	heard [ɜ:]	heard [ɜ:]	sit	sat	sat
break	broke	broken	hide	hid	hidden	sleep	slept	slept
bring	brought	brought	hit	hit	hit	smell	smelt	smelt
build	built	built	hold	held	held		smelled†	smelled
burn	burnt	burnt	hurt	hurt	hurt	speak	spoke	spoken
	burned†	burned	keep	kept	kept	spell	spelt	spelt
burst	burst	burst	know	knew	known		spelled†	spelled
buy	bought	bought	lay	laid	laid	spend	spent	spent
catch	caught	caught	lead	led	led	spoil	spoilt	spoilt
choose	chose	chosen	learn	learnt	learnt		spoiled†	spoiled
come	came	come		learned†	learned	spread	spread	spread
cost	cost	cost	leave	left	left	spring	sprang	sprung
cut	cut	cut	lend	lent	lent	stand	stood	stood
deal [i:]	dealt [e]	dealt [e]	let	let	let	steal	stole	stolen
dig	dug	dug	lie	lay	lain	stick	stuck	stuck
do (does [ʌ])	did	done	light	lighted/lit	lighted/lit	sting	stung	stung
draw	drew	drawn	lose	lost	lost	stink	stank/stunk	stunk
dream [i:]	dreamed [i:]	dreamed [i:]	make	made	made	strike	struck	struck
	dreamt [e]	dreamt [e]	mean [i:]	meant [e]	meant [e]	sweep	swept	swept
drink	drank	drunk	meet	met	met	swim	swam	swum
drive	drove	driven	pay	paid	paid	swing	swung	swung
eat [i:]	ate [et]	eaten [i:]	put	put	put	take	took	taken
	[eɪt] (USA)		read [i:]	read [e]	read [e]	teach	taught	taught
fall	fell	fallen	ride	rode	ridden	tear	tore	torn
feed	fed	fed	ring	rang	rung	tell	told	told
feel	felt	felt	rise	rose	risen	think	thought	thought
fight	fought	fought	run	ran	run	throw	threw	thrown
find	found	found	say [eɪ]	said [e]	said [e]	understand	understood	understood
flee	fled	fled	(says [e])			wake	woke	woken
fly	flew	flown	see	saw	seen		waked	waked
forbid	forbade [æ]	forbidden	seek	sought	sought	wear	wore	worn
	forbad		sell	sold	sold	win	won	won
forget	forgot	forgotten	send	sent	sent	write	wrote	written

* and irregular simple present forms   † Some verbs have two past forms, e.g. *learnt/learned*. The form with *-t* is more usual in British English and the form with *-ed* in American English. *burned, learned, smelled, spelled* and *spoiled* can be pronounced with [t] or [d].

Glossary

This glossary gives the meaning of the grammatical terms used in this book.

active ▷ **passive**

adjective In the sentence *It's a big house*, the word *big* is an adjective. An adjective is used to describe a noun. ▷ 23.1

adverb In the sentence *She was speaking quietly*, the word *quietly* is an adverb. ▷ 24

adverb phrase a phrase which we use like an adverb, e.g. *I found it **with some difficulty**. They came **yesterday morning**.*

agent the person or thing that does the action ▷ 10.2

alternative question a question with the word *or*, e.g. *Do you want a large one or a small one?*

apostrophe In the phrase *my sister's book*, there is an apostrophe between *sister* and *s*. ▷ 39.5

apposition In the sentence *Do you know Don Burgess, the actor?* the noun phrases *Don Burgess* and *the actor* are in apposition. ▷ 18.16

article *a/an* and *the* ▷ 19

auxiliary verb helping verb: *be, have* and *do* ▷ 5.1. See also **modal verb**.

base form the simple form of the verb without -ing, -ed or -s, e.g. *go, play*

cardinal numbers *one, two, three* etc. are cardinal numbers. *first, second, third* etc. are ordinal numbers.

clause In the sentence *We can go in the car if it rains*, there are two clauses – *We can go in the car* and *if it rains*. ▷ **main clause, sub clause**

collective noun a noun used to refer to a group, e.g. *family, crowd* ▷ 18.14

comparative *smaller* and *more interesting* are the comparative forms of the adjectives *small* and *interesting*.

comparison the comparing of two or more things with forms like *longer, most exciting, as quickly as*

complement In the sentence *She's a doctor*, the phrase *a doctor* is the complement. The complement is used to describe the subject. Sometimes an object has a complement; in the sentence *They made him captain*, the word *captain* is the complement.

compound a word formed from two or more other words, e.g. *milkman* (milk + man), *somewhere* (some + where), *ten-year-old*

conjunction a word used to join two clauses, e.g. *and, but, or, when, if, because* ▷ **vowel**

consonant ▷ **vowel**

continuous a verb form with *be* and the -ing form, e.g. *He **was working**.*

countable noun a noun which can have a plural form. *book, coat* and *plate* are countable nouns. ▷ **uncountable**

defining relative clause e.g. *That's the man **who won the prize**.* ▷ 22.12

definite *ten minutes* is a definite time; we know how many minutes. *a few minutes* is an indefinite time; we do not know exactly how many minutes.

degree *very, rather* and *almost* are adverbs of degree. ▷ 24.8

demonstrative adjective/pronoun *this, that, these* and *those* ▷ 20.12

direct object In the sentence *The boy gave his father a book*, the noun phrase *a book* is the direct object, and the noun phrase *his father* is the indirect object.

direct speech ▷ **reported speech**

-ed form ▷ **past participle**

emphasis greater stress or importance

given to a word or phrase ▷ 28. (Adjective: **emphatic**)

emphatic pronoun e.g. *He built the house **himself**.* ▷ 20.9

ending In the noun *rooms*, -s is the plural ending.

end position In the sentence *We go out sometimes*, the word *sometimes* is in end position. ▷ 24.4

exclamation words spoken suddenly and with feeling, e.g. *Stop! How beautiful!* ▷ 34.1

falling intonation the voice going down ▷ **intonation**

formal Friendly, everyday conversations and personal letters to friends are informal. Business letters and polite conversations with strangers are more formal.

frequency how often something happens. *sometimes* and *often* are adverbs of frequency. ▷ 24.7

front position In the sentence *Sometimes we go out*, the word *sometimes* is in front position. ▷ 24.4

future the time that has not yet come, the time after now

imperative the base form of a verb used to give orders etc., e.g. ***Wait** a minute. **Come** here.* ▷ 6.1

indefinite ▷ **definite**

indirect object ▷ **direct object**

infinitive the base form of a verb, e.g. *wait, come*. The infinitive often has *to* in front of it, e.g. *to wait, to come*. ▷ 14

informal ▷ **formal**

-ing form form of a verb with -ing, e.g. *opening, walking* ▷ **present participle, verbal noun**

intonation the speaker's voice going up and down. We normally use a falling intonation in a statement (e.g. *It's half past five*) and a rising intonation in a yes/no question (e.g. *Is it half past five?*).

irregular ▷ **regular**

linking word a conjunction (e.g. *and, when*) or a word or phrase which makes a link between two sentences, e.g. *therefore, on the other hand* ▷ 27

main clause In the sentence *I was there when it happened, I was there* is the main clause and *when it happened* is a sub clause. Every sentence has a main clause, and sometimes a sentence is a main clause only. A main clause usually has a subject and verb.

main verb the verb in the main clause. In the sentence *I stopped because I was tired, stopped* is the main verb.

manner *nicely, angrily* and *strangely* are adverbs of manner. ▷ 24.5

mid position In the sentence *We sometimes go out*, the word *sometimes* is in mid position. ▷ 24.4

modal verb (or **modal auxiliary verb**) The modal verbs are *can, could, may, might, will, would, shall, should, ought to, must, need* and *dare*.

negative A sentence with *n't* or *not* or with *no, neither* etc. is negative, e.g. *I haven't got a watch. Are there no eggs?* Other sentences are positive, e.g. *I've got a watch.*

non-defining relative clause e.g. *Alex, who came first*, won the prize. ▷ 22.12

normal verb an ordinary verb (e.g. *look, come*), not an auxiliary or modal verb

noun In the sentence *The chair is in the garden*, the words *chair* and *garden* are nouns.

noun phrase a phrase which can be the subject or object of a sentence, e.g. *my bag, these old clothes*

object ▷ **direct object**

ordinal numbers ▷ **cardinal numbers**

pair noun a noun which is always plural in form and can be used with *pair of*, e.g. *trousers, scissors* ▷ 18.12

participle ▷ **present participle, past participle**

passive *The police arrested the man* is an active sentence. *The man was arrested* is a passive sentence. ▷ 10.1

past the time that is already over, the time before now

past continuous a tense with *was/were* and the -ing form, e.g. *I was washing my hair.* ▷ 3.7

past participle the -ed form of a verb, e.g. *opened, walked*; some forms are irregular, e.g. *seen, come*

past perfect a tense with *had* and the -ed form, e.g. *The concert had already started.* ▷ 3.6

past perfect continuous a tense with *had been* and the -ing form, e.g. *He was hot because he had been running.* ▷ 3.10

perception *see, hear* and *smell* are verbs of perception.

perfect a verb form with *have* and the -ed form, e.g. *They had already arrived.*

person 1st person = *I, we*; 2nd person = *you*; 3rd person = *he, she, it, they*

personal pronoun e.g. *I, me, you, he, him* ▷ 20.1

phrasal-prepositional verb a verb + adverb + preposition, e.g. *Keep away from the edge of the cliff.*

phrasal verb a verb + adverb, e.g. *Let's wash up. Take your coat off.* ▷ 26.1

phrase a group of words but not a full clause or sentence, e.g. *the small box* (a noun phrase), *is going* (a verb phrase), *very often* (an adverb phrase)

plural a form used to talk about more than one thing. *dogs* is the plural of *dog*. ▷ **singular**

positive ▷ **negative**

possessive a form used to show that something belongs to somebody, e.g. *Peter's, ours*

possessive adjective e.g. *my, your, his, her* ▷ 20.5

possessive pronoun e.g. *mine, yours, his, hers* ▷ 20.5

prefix something added to the beginning of a word to change the meaning, e.g. *unfair, re-open*

preposition e.g. *in, on, under, at, to* ▷ 25

prepositional adverb an adverb which is like a preposition but has no noun phrase after it, e.g. *A man went past.*

prepositional verb a verb + preposition, e.g. *Let's listen to the news. We laughed at the joke.* ▷ 26.3

present the time now, at this moment

present continuous a tense with *am/are/is* and the -ing form, e.g. *I'm making the dinner.* ▷ 2.3

present participle the -ing form of a verb when used as an adjective or adverb or in a continuous tense form. The -ing forms in these sentences are present participles; *He jumped from the moving train. They ate standing up. The girl was sleeping.*

present perfect a tense with *has/have* and the -ed form, e.g. *We've finished.* ▷ 3.4

present perfect continuous a tense with *has been/have been* and the -ing form, e.g. *I've been waiting for ages.* ▷ 3.8

pronoun e.g. *you, it, mine* ▷ 20

pronounce say words correctly (Noun: **pronunciation**)

punctuation A comma (,) and a full stop (.) are punctuation marks.

quantifier a word that tells us about quantity (how many or how much), e.g. *some, every, enough*

question tag e.g. *It's Monday today, isn't it?* ▷ 8.5

question word *what, who, where, when, why, how* and *whose* are question words ▷ 21

reflexive pronoun e.g. *I've hurt **myself**.*
▷ 20.8

regular the same as most others. *boys* and *girls* are nouns with regular plural endings in *-s*. *children* is an irregular plural form.

relative clause e.g. *That's the girl **who lost her money**.* ▷ 22

relative pronoun In the sentence *The man who spoke to you is a detective*, the word *who* is a relative pronoun. We can use *who, which, that, whose, whom* and *what* as relative pronouns. ▷ 22

reported speech The sentence *'I can come'* is direct speech. In the sentence *He says he can come*, the clause *he can come* is reported speech. ▷ 12.1

reporting verb a verb used to report speech or thoughts, e.g. *say, tell, ask, think, mention* ▷ 12.1

rising intonation the voice going up ▷ **intonation**

sentence A sentence is one or more clauses. It can be a statement, a question, an order or an exclamation. A written sentence begins with a capital letter and ends with a full stop (.), question mark (?) or exclamation mark (!).

sentence adverb an adverb that refers to a whole sentence, e.g. ***Luckily**, no one was hurt.* ▷ 24.9

short answer e.g. *Yes, he was. No, I'm not. Yes, you can.*

short form e.g. *you're, they'll, isn't* ▷ 39.6

simple past a verb tense, e.g. *I **washed** the floor yesterday.* ▷ 3.3

simple present a verb tense, e.g. *I **see** him every day.* ▷ 2.4

singular a form used to talk about one thing only. *cup* is singular; *cups* is plural.

spelling how words are written

statement a sentence which gives information, e.g. *It's raining. The meat is very good*; not a question or an order.

stress the speaking of a word (or part of a word) more loudly than other words. In the word *remember*, the stress is on the second syllable – *re'member*.

sub clause e.g. *I'll give it you **when I see you**. **If she comes**, I can meet her. Is that the man **who you spoke to**? Someone said **that it was ready**.* A sub clause (= subordinate clause) usually begins with a conjunction, e.g. *when, if, that*, or with a relative pronoun. It cannot stand alone as a sentence like the main clause. It usually has a subject and verb, but it can be an -ing form or infinitive without a subject, e.g. ***Coming out of the shop**, I suddenly felt ill. You need a hammer **to do that**.*

subject In the sentence *The man opened the door*, the noun phrase *the man* is the subject.

superlative *smallest* and *most interesting* are the superlative forms of the adjectives *small* and *interesting*.

syllable The word *information* has four syllables (*in for ma tion*).

tag ▷ **question tag**

tense a form of the verb which tells us when something happens, e.g. in the present, the past or the future

uncountable noun a noun which cannot have a plural form. *butter, coffee* and *oil* are uncountable nouns.

verb In the sentence *I go to work by bus*, the word *go* is a verb.

verbal noun the -ing form of a verb when used as a noun, e.g. *I like **reading**.*

verb of perception e.g. *see, hear, smell*

verb phrase either a verb on its own (e.g. *I **was** hungry. We **played** cards.*) or a verb with an auxiliary and/or modal verb (e.g. *They **were singing**. She **must have gone** home.*)

voiced/voiceless Voiced sounds are all the vowel sounds (e.g. [iː], [e], [aʊ]) and the consonant sounds [b], [d], [g], [z], [ʒ], [dʒ], [v], [ð], [l], [r], [m], [n], and [ŋ]. Voiceless sounds are the consonant sounds [p], [t], [k], [s], [ʃ], [tʃ], [f] and [θ].

vowel The letters *a, e, i, o* and *u* are vowels. The other letters are consonants.

wh- question a question that begins with a question word, e.g. *What/Who/Whose . . .?*

yes/no question a question that we can answer with yes or no

Index